ZACK HAMPLE

WATCHING BASEBALL SMARTER

Zack Hample, arguably one of the more serious geeks, is obsessed with the National Pastime. A former college third baseman and four-time student at Bucky Dent's Baseball School, Hample has worked as both a baseball instructor and a spokesman. He is best known for having collected an obscene number of baseballs—2,961 and counting—at forty-one major league stadiums, including Barry Bonds's 724th career home run. His first book, *How to Snag Major League Baseballs,* was published in 1999, landing him coverage in *Sports Illustrated, People, Playboy, The New York Times, The Canadian National Post, FHM, Parade* magazine, *Time for Kids,* and on National Public Radio, CNN, FOX Sports, *The Rosie O'Donnell Show,* and the *CBS Evening News with Katie Couric.* Hample, a New York City native, currently writes for minorleaguebaseball.com and has a popular blog, "The Baseball Collector," about his favorite hobby. He has other interests, of course; they just aren't evident during baseball season.

www.zackhample.com

ALSO BY ZACK HAMPLE

How to Snag Major League Baseballs

WATCHING
BASEBALL
SMARTER

*A Professional Fan's Guide for Beginners,
Semi-experts, and Deeply Serious Geeks*

ZACK HAMPLE

Vintage Books
A Division of Random House, Inc.
New York

A VINTAGE ORIGINAL, MARCH 2007

Cataloging-in-Publication Data is on file at the Library of Congress.

Vintage ISBN: 978-0-307-28032-9

Illustrations by Laura Hartman Maestro

Book design by Robert Bull

www.vintagebooks.com

Printed in the United States of America

10 9 8 7 6 5 4 3

*To my father's father, Benny Hample—the one grandparent
I never met and the biggest baseball fan of all.*

CONTENTS

CHAPTER 3. **HITTING**

CHAPTER 4. **BASERUNNING**

CHAPTER 5. **FIELDING**

CHAPTER 6. STADIUMS

CHAPTER 7. UMPIRES

CHAPTER 8. **STATISTICS**

CHAPTER 9. **RANDOM STUFF TO KNOW**

CHAPTER 10. **RANDOM STUFF TO NOTICE**

PREFACE

Baseball is like church. Many attend, but few understand.

—Wes Westrum, former major league catcher

This is not the only book about watching and understanding baseball, but it is the only one that explains, among other things, why players are always grabbing their crotches (see Chapter 9, "Grab *This*"). I know why they do because I've done it myself. I did it from Little League to college, and in between I did it at countless baseball camps and clinics from Florida to Canada.

I don't mean to brag. It's not like I ever got to do it on national television, and anyway, it's nothing to be proud of. But then again, it's nothing to be ashamed of either. It's just part of the game, and that's why you'll find it here. That's why you'll find sections about steroids, statistics, salaries, surgeries, stadiums, superstitions, and spitting. These things are also part of the game. Are they peripheral? No doubt. But in order to appreciate baseball—to be a true fan or at least fool the die-hards—you need to know about them.

Most fans know that the batter is awarded first base when he gets hit by a pitch. But most fans don't know exactly how much it hurts. They don't know the story of the only guy who was killed by a pitch, they can't tell you the first team to wear helmets, and they have no idea when the single earflap became a required addition. Yeah, this stuff is dorky, but it's part of the fun. Instead of reading a brief explanation of the infield fly rule and stopping there, why not learn a few obscure facts about it? That way, when some baseball snob tries to test your knowledge by throwing it in your face, you'll have a little ammunition to throw back.

"Why, yes, as a matter of fact I have heard of the infield fly rule, and do *you* know what year it was instituted?"

If you hang around baseball fans, someone *will* challenge you. Believe me. I know how fans think because I am one. I've memorized the stats on way too many of my 100,000 cards, I've waited in the rain for some of my 1,500 autographs, and I've strategically planned my trips to the bathroom at all of the 41 major league stadiums I've visited. (Don't wait for the third out—everyone else will be there too.)

Watching baseball in person is certainly exciting, but it's not the best way to learn the game. Unless you're lucky enough to be there with an expert, there's no one to explain the context, the characters, the lingo, the lore, the history, the strategy, the behind-the-scenes stuff, and, most importantly, the nuance—and if you're not lucky enough to have box seats, you won't be close enough to see it anyway.

I prefer watching baseball on TV. I like that it's free and that the view is always good, even from the bathroom if the set is positioned just right. I also like the different camera angles and slow-motion instant replays—you won't see many of those on the JumboTron, especially on close calls that go against the home team, because stadium management would rather prevent a riot than entertain the crowd—but most of all, I like to listen to the announcers.

Most announcers work in pairs. A hotshot sports anchor—the "play-by-play guy"—usually describes the action alongside a former player—the "color commentator"—who fills the gaps with anecdotes and insider analysis. It's great for seasoned fans, but for those who don't live for the sport, it can be confusing, particularly when the announcers use slang:

"Johnson chokes up and tomahawks a Baltimore Chop off the dish, but Rodriguez charges, scoops the in-between hop in the 5.5-hole, and hoses him at first on a bang-bang play!"

Huh?

It's a fancy way of saying that the batter grounded out to the shortstop. Baseball embraces colorful language. You need to understand it.

Throughout this book you'll see slang and key terms in *italics*. If you don't know what something means, check out the glossary. It's meant to be interactive—in some places it might take a minute to flip back and forth—but with hundreds of terms that don't appear anywhere else in the book, it also stands as its own section. I suggest that you read the glossary straight through, but if that's a drag, at least keep it bookmarked beside your TV or radio so you can look things up when the announcers are showing off.

The first time I showed this book to a group of friends—fans of all levels—I had hoped that it would appeal to all of them. I'd covered the basics. I'd examined the esoteric. It was funny. It was serious. There were stats and anecdotes. There was history and strategy. It was well rounded and—

"You need to explain more," said a young woman. "I don't know what a ground ball is."

She wasn't kidding. I'd been through this before. I once spent two hours explaining baseball—from scratch—to some dude from England. He'd never seen the sport, not even a glimpse on TV.

"Okay now, see the guy standing over there holding the long piece of wood? That's the batter."

And that's how the lesson began—but it's not how I've written this book, so I hope you already know how many outs are in an inning and how many innings are in a game. I hope you know where home plate is. I hope you know what you call the guy who stands there with the long piece of wood. And I hope you know the definition of a ground ball. After all, I talk about them quite a bit, and there are many types. (It's kind of like how the Eskimos have various words for snow.) You need to be able to visualize a routine grounder before you can distinguish the squibbers from the squirters, the screamers from the scorchers, the nubbers from the huggers, the dribblers from the bleeders, the rollers from the tappers, and the room service hops from the Baltimore Chops.

But don't worry about your baseball knowledge. Seriously. If you've ever swung a bat or watched an inning here and there, you'll be fine. And if you already know everything, you'll find stuff you didn't know.

My parents fall somewhere in the middle. Way back in the day, my dad was a ball boy for a minor league team that had a future Hall-of-Fame pitcher named Warren Spahn, and in the more recent past my mom routinely outslugged all other moms in family softball games. They know a thing or two about the sport, but they're not experts, so I wrote the book with them in mind. They inspired it by asking so many questions when we watched big games together: What does the coach talk about on the mound? Is this guy any good? How did you know he was going to throw a curveball? What's the Mendoza line? Did he hit him on purpose? What's the deal with that pattern in the outfield grass? How many balls are used each game? Why are umps so fat? Can you please explain slugging percentage again? Why does the catcher keep looking off to the side? How do you throw a knuckle-ball? And c'mon, why *are* they always grabbing their crotches?

It seemed logical that other fans probably questioned the same things—and more.

Here are the answers.

WATCHING
BASEBALL
SMARTER

CHAPTER 1
THE BASICS

There's one word that describes baseball: "You never know."
—Joaquin Andujar, former major league pitcher

THE DREAM

Life is pretty good if you're in the Major Leagues. First of all, you get to hang out with other major leaguers. You also get to be on TV every day and play in front of thousands of people. You get to see your name in newspapers and magazines and on the back of people's T-shirts. You get to see your face on scoreboards and baseball cards and posters. You get free equipment from sporting goods companies. You get unlimited bubble gum and sunflower seeds in the dugout. You get to relax in the clubhouse and watch big-screen TVs from fancy leather couches while other people get paid to wash your uniform. You get to fly on private jets and stay in nice hotels. You get recognized by kids and pretty women who scream for autographs. Sometimes old men scream too. You earn an average annual salary of $2.9 million (or roughly $17,900 per game), and when the team travels, you get over $75 extra every day to spend on food.

No wonder the dream starts early.

But is it simply about fame and money? Maybe it's about having the chance to do something spectacular in one instant that people will always remember. Maybe it's about a subconscious desire to play a game full-time and act like a little boy well into adulthood. Maybe it's about having the manager and trainer race onto the field to make sure you're okay after you hit a foul ball off your ankle.

The motivation is almost irrelevant because every kid with the dream wants it bad. Every kid has a reason. Every kid has a story. Every kid has a good baseball name. Every kid practices his swing in the mirror. Every kid can steal a base and catch a fly ball and throw strikes. Every kid converts his statistics into a 600-at-bat season and concludes that he'll be a superstar in the majors. Every kid is sure he's gonna make it—and 99,999 out of 100,000 kids are wrong. They don't know how much better the competition gets every step of the way. They don't know how long the journey takes. They don't know that there's always some other kid with an edge. Someone is always taller, stronger, faster, smarter. Someone has quicker feet and softer hands and sharper eyes and better instincts. Someone runs more. Someone lifts weights more. Someone is using steroids. Someone's father is a baseball coach. Someone's older brother is already playing pro ball. Someone has a batting tee in the basement or a batting cage in the backyard. Someone lives in warmer weather and gets to practice year-round. Someone wants it more than anyone on earth has ever wanted it.

There's T-ball, Wiffle ball, softball, and Little League. There are baseball camps, baseball schools, private lessons, and winter clinics in stuffy gymnasiums. There's high school ball, college ball, summer ball, and fall ball. There's Babe Ruth League, the Cape Cod League, semipro leagues, and *independent leagues*. There are scouts, agents, tryouts, strikeouts, errors, cuts, injuries, surgeries, and lifelong dreams that can die in an instant.

But every year, the dream stays alive for 1,500 young men, at least for a little while, when they're selected by major league *organizations* in the *First-Year Player Draft*.

THE DRAFT

Basketball players used to jump directly from high school to the NBA. Football players push right through college to the NFL. But baseball players have it much harder—as do the scouts who discover them. Almost all players start their careers in the Minor Leagues because their talent is less predictable and takes longer to develop.

Each June the ongoing search for talent begins a new cycle with the 50-round draft. Every major league team employs dozens of scouts who focus on North American players— mostly high school and college graduates—who are eligible for the draft. Now that baseball is spreading internationally, scouts also comb the rest of the globe for prospects who can sign outside of the draft as *free agents* if they're at least 16 years old. But the draft supplies more future major leaguers than any other talent pool.

Teams are assigned an order for selecting players, based on the previous season's won-lost records. The lousier teams get the higher picks. (Some people wonder if teams prefer to finish last once the season starts going downhill.)

The draft serves two purposes: to distribute the talent evenly and to keep signing bonuses from surging. Players are not free agents in the draft. They are forced to negotiate only with the team that selects them. If a player refuses an offer, he must wait a year and reenter the draft.

Even though every kid dreams of playing in the big leagues, it's not always easy for a team to complete the deal with a player it has drafted. For example, a high school star who's offered a $10,000 signing bonus for his 16th-round selection might also have heard from dozens of colleges that offered him full scholarships and a chance to play on their *Division I* teams. He may choose to stay in school, knowing that his skills could improve so much in four years that he might eventually be a first-round draft pick and earn a multimillion-dollar signing bonus. And if his future professional team pays him that much, the organization will stick with him if he struggles and give him all the instruction, attention, and support he needs to reach the majors.

Scouts look for intangibles like maturity, aggressiveness, and baseball instincts. When it comes to finding *position players,* a scout's Holy Grail is the *five-tool player,* the five tools being the ability to field well, throw hard, run fast, hit home runs, and hit for a high *batting average.* Barry Bonds, in his prime, was the ultimate five-tool player.

With pitchers, scouts look for velocity and accuracy, but they don't just want throwers; they want pitchers who use their heads and have a game plan. Left-handers are always in demand because their pitches naturally have more *movement*—no one's really sure why—and because they're more effective against left-handed hitters. Teams seek tall pitchers, not only because their big bodies are more durable, but because their long arms allow them to release the ball closer to home plate, giving hitters less time to react. Tall guys also have better *leverage,* meaning their higher release points allow them to throw with a greater downward angle for more velocity. Look at any team's roster and you'll notice that there aren't many players—especially pitchers— under six feet tall.[1]

THE ROAD TO THE MAJOR LEAGUES

Of the tens of thousands of players selected since the draft began in 1965, fewer than two dozen have jumped directly to the majors. Mike Adamson became the first in 1967 when the Baltimore Orioles plucked him from the University of Southern California. Dave Winfield is the lone Hall of Famer on the list, but there are other big names, such as Burt Hooton, Dick Ruthven, Mike Morgan, Bob Horner, Pete Incaviglia, John Olerud, Chan Ho Park, and one-handed pitcher Jim Abbott.

Everyone else faces the ugly reality of life in the Minor Leagues. During *homestands,* some players live with host families who volunteer through their teams. On the road, all players endure endless bus rides, stay at cheap hotels, and receive a measly $20 a day for meals. They earn a maximum of $850 per month during their first season at the bottom of the professional baseball totem pole—and most of them couldn't be happier.

Most teams' minor league systems have these six levels, each divided into several leagues:

LEVEL	LEAGUE NAMES
Rookie	Appalachian, Arizona, Gulf Coast, Pioneer
Class A Short-Season	New York–Penn, Northwest
Class A	Midwest, South Atlantic
Class A Advanced	California, Carolina, Florida State
Double-A	Eastern, Southern, Texas
Triple-A	International, Pacific Coast

[1]The shortest player in major league history is Eddie Gaedel, a 3-foot-7 midget used as a promotional stunt by St. Louis Browns owner Bill Veeck against the Detroit Tigers on August 19, 1951. Wearing uniform number 1/8 for his only appearance, the 65-pound Gaedel walked on four straight pitches and was promptly replaced at first base by a *pinchrunner.* Two days later the league barred him from playing again.

The Detroit Tigers, for example, have a Rookie team in the Gulf Coast League, a Class A Short-Season team in the New York–Penn League, a Class A team in the Midwest League, a Class A Advanced team in the Florida State League, a Double-A team in the Eastern League, and a Triple-A team in the International League.

When advancing to Triple-A, the highest level before the majors, players face a significant competitive jump because the rosters include many former major leaguers (and current ones recovering from injuries on *rehab assignments*) who are trying to get back to *The Show*.

Skipping a higher level of the Minor Leagues is rare; most players advance one level at a time only after demonstrating that they're better than most of the competition. So think twice before you yell, "He stinks!" about any major leaguer; he's spent his entire life beating the odds and proving himself as the best of the best of the best of the best of the best.

Players and scouts often mention that it's more difficult to make it from the minors to the majors than it is to get drafted in the first place. Of the minor leaguers who do reach the majors, many get just a *cup of coffee* before fading into oblivion—but even they get their names in the *Baseball Encyclopedia*. Most minor leaguers never make it and get released when their organizations give up on them (if they don't get discouraged and quit on their own). Still, they'll always be able to say that they played professional baseball.

LEAGUES, DIVISIONS, AND TEAMS

Major League Baseball (MLB) has 30 teams and two leagues. The National League (NL) and American League (AL) each have three divisions called the East, Central, and West. Take a look at the breakdown:

NL EAST	NL CENTRAL	NL WEST
Atlanta Braves	Chicago Cubs	Arizona Diamondbacks
Florida Marlins	Cincinnati Reds	Colorado Rockies
New York Mets	Houston Astros	Los Angeles Dodgers
Philadelphia Phillies	Milwaukee Brewers	San Diego Padres
Washington Nationals	Pittsburgh Pirates	San Francisco Giants
	St. Louis Cardinals	

AL EAST	AL CENTRAL	AL WEST
Baltimore Orioles	Chicago White Sox	Los Angeles Angels of Anaheim
Boston Red Sox	Cleveland Indians	Oakland Athletics[2]
New York Yankees	Detroit Tigers	Seattle Mariners
Tampa Bay Devil Rays	Kansas City Royals	Texas Rangers
Toronto Blue Jays	Minnesota Twins	

Before 1997, teams played only within their league during the *regular season*. Then baseball officials introduced *interleague* play. The new matchups, though limited to just a handful of games each year, boosted attendance but angered purists who felt that the *World Series* should have remained the only meeting between the leagues. Many people think it's odd that the NL has two more teams than the AL, but if each had 15, the odd number would force one team in each league to either play an interleague game or take a day off every day.

[2]Don't call them the "Athletics." Baseball fans will laugh at you. Call them the "A's" instead. That's just how they're known. Other teams do have nicknames (Cardinals/Redbirds, Angels/Halos, White Sox/Pale Hose, Padres/Friars, Diamondbacks/D'backs, etc.), but they're not used with such regularity.

The major difference between the leagues is the *designated hitter* (*DH*). In the National League, the pitcher, like everyone else who plays the field, has a spot in the batting order. In the American League, the DH bats for him. In interleague play, All-Star Games, and the World Series, the home team's ballpark determines the DH rule. Why does the AL have a DH? Good question. After fans supposedly got bored seeing pitchers dominate the sport in the 1960s, the American League adopted the DH in 1973 to bolster offense and attendance; the National League voted against it and still drew more fans than the AL.

(In order to call yourself a baseball fan, you must have an opinion on the designated hitter; you either love that it creates more offense by replacing weak-hitting pitchers with full-time sluggers or you hate that it eliminates the late-inning strategy of dealing with those pitchers. If a guy is pitching well, should the manager let him bat in a crucial situation so he can return to the mound for another inning or two? Or should the manager use a *pinch-hitter* and turn the ball over to the *bullpen*? These decisions don't exist in the AL.)

SPRING TRAINING

After each dreary off-season, baseball comes back to life in mid-February when pitchers and catchers report to *Spring Training*. All other players show up five days later because, quite simply, their positions are less demanding and don't require the extra work.

In the old days, players used Spring Training to get in shape for the regular season. Nowadays, everyone arrives in top physical condition. Superstars want to prove that they deserve their salaries, while many other players compete to make the team and avoid beginning the season in the minors.

There's no NL or AL in the preseason (but the home team still determines the DH rule). Instead, 18 of the 30 major league teams, mostly from the East and Central Divisions, play in Florida in the *Grapefruit League*. The other 12 teams, mostly from the West, play in Arizona in the *Cactus League*.

THE REGULAR SEASON

For most teams, the 162-game *regular season* begins on the first Monday in April and ends either on the last Sunday in September or the first in October. Major League Baseball uses an *unbalanced schedule,* which means that teams don't all face each other the same number of times. Instead, they play more games within their divisions. Teams sometimes complain that their road trips are too long, that they don't play a particular divisional rival until July, or that they lose money when the popular matchups take place in the other team's ballpark. Too bad. The schedule makers organize 2,430 games each season and can't please everyone.

Teams don't always finish the season having played exactly 162 games. They may play one fewer when a meaningless late-season contest gets rained out and can't be rescheduled. Or if two teams are tied after 162 games with one postseason slot remaining, there are certain circumstances that would force an extra one-game playoff, creating a rare 163-game season.

THE POSTSEASON

Let's start from the beginning. The first World Series was played in 1903 as a best-of-nine contest, and the Boston Americans (who became the Red Sox five years later) beat the Pittsburgh Pirates five games to three. All other World Series have been best-of-seven, except those from 1919 to 1921, which reverted to the original format. The Series used to be the only postseason matchup; there were no divisions, so the first-place teams in each league played each other after the regular season and *wham!* that was it.

Divisional play began in 1969 when the leagues divided into East and West. This created another round in the postseason called the *League Championship Series* (LCS) and allowed four teams to compete: the first-place team in the NL East played the first-place team in the NL West in the NLCS, and the two first-place teams in the AL played in the ALCS. The two winners then faced off in the World Series.

The LCS switched from best-of-five to best-of-seven in 1985. Seven-game series follow a two-three-two format. That means the team with the home-field advantage (usually the squad with more wins during the regular season) plays the first two games at its home field, the next three at its opponent's stadium, and the final two—if the series hasn't already ended—back home.

Team owners realized that more playoff games meant more money, so in 1994 they realigned each league into three divisions—East, Central, and West—to create an additional round. This allowed six first-place teams and two *Wild Card* teams— the best second-place teams from each league—to participate, and the new format caused an uproar. Critics claimed that baseball, by allowing more teams to reach the playoffs, was rewarding mediocrity like the other major sports did.

Sport	Total Teams	Playoff Teams	Percentage Reaching Playoffs
Basketball (NBA)	30	16	53.33
Hockey (NHL)	30	16	53.33
Football (NFL)	32	12	37.50
Baseball (MLB)	30	8	26.67

Supporters argued that it was still a challenge to reach the playoffs and that the fans and players were happier because more teams remained competitive late in the season. Regardless, this round is called the *League Division Series* (LDS). It's best-of-five and follows a two-two-one format, and most people have grown to love it.[3]

---

[3]"Most people" includes everyone except Braves fans, many of whom became so spoiled by watching their team win 14 consecutive division titles—a record in professional sports—from 1991 to 2005 that Atlanta's Turner Field often failed to sell out until the NLCS.

CHAPTER 2

PITCHERS AND CATCHERS

I remember one time going out to the mound to talk with Bob Gibson. He told me to get back behind the batter, that the only thing I knew about pitching was that it was hard to hit.

—Tim McCarver, former major league catcher

WAIT FOR YOUR PITCH!

Doesn't it look stupid when a major league hitter watches a pitch sail through the middle of the strike zone before swinging at the next one, which bounces in the dirt? For $2.9 million, you could do just as good a job. Hell, you'd do it for half of that.

We've all felt this way because, at least a few times in our lives, we've all held a baseball bat and swung furiously at a little round thing thrown our way. And ever since we were old enough to stand, we've been told, "Keep your eye on the ball," and "Wait for your pitch."

It sounds easy, and for some of us it is. Most of our bat-swinging has come against a friend who lobs one pitch after another, or a kid whose pitches barely reach home plate. We have plenty of time to gauge the direction and trajectory of the pitch, to think about what we're having for dinner, and to decide if we want to swing. Timing is not even a factor because all the pitches travel at the same speed. And still, we sometimes chase balls out of the strike zone.

Why does a major league hitter do the same thing? Because the ball comes in so fast that he has to guess what type of pitch is coming and base his decision to swing on the beginning of its path toward home plate. Many pitches appear to be heading for the strike zone before sinking or curving out of it, while others start outside the zone before making a late break and earning a called strike from the ump. So when you see a hitter swing at a bad pitch or watch a good one, feel free to yell at him, but keep in mind that all he did was guess wrong against one of the world's best pitchers who has spent his entire life preparing to strike him out.

Wade Boggs, a perennial batting champion for the Red Sox in the 1980s, took the phrase *good eye* to a new level. He didn't always have to guess because he had better than 20/20 vision and could identify certain pitches by the way the ball left the pitcher's hand. Other hitters can determine the types of pitches by their spin. But for normal human beings, the challenge is greater. Here's what hitters face when they step into the batter's box:

FASTBALL (aka *heater, hummer, dead red, cheese, smoke, gas, swifty, express, number one*)—Generally traveling 86 to 98 miles per hour and reaching home plate in 0.4 seconds, fastballs are the most common pitch and the easiest to control because of the comfortable grip and standard release. There are five variations:

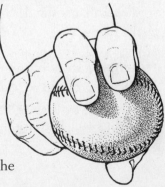

- A *four-seam fastball* (aka *four-seamer, cross-seam fastball*) is held with the fingers across the widest part of the seams and travels straight because of the consistent rotation and air resistance.

- A *two-seam fastball* (aka *two-seamer, tailing fastball*) is held with the index and middle fingers atop the seams at their narrowest point and moves toward the side of the plate from which the pitcher throws. (It tails inside to a righty when thrown by a righty.)

- A *cut fastball* (aka *cutter*) has the opposite lateral movement of a two-seamer; it moves toward the opposite side of the plate from which the pitcher throws. If a right-handed pitcher successfully throws it inside to a lefty, he can *jam* the hitter and break his bat.

- A *sinker* is held like the two-seamer, but with the thumb directly underneath the ball. It's thrown a bit slower than a standard fastball and drops as it reaches the plate.

- A *rising fastball* is thrown so hard that it appears to take off as it crosses the plate near the top of the strike zone. Even though it's almost impossible to hit, the batter might swing because the ball looks like a bigger target near eye level.

CURVEBALL (aka *bender, deuce, hammer, hook, Uncle Charlie, Lord Charles, yakker, snapper, Mr. Snappy, number two*)— Baseballs are handmade, so they're not all exactly the same. Most variations (size, weight, shape, density, etc.) are negligible and don't affect the game, but one difference stands out enough to make the pitcher happy: raised seams. When throwing a curve, anywhere from 10 to 20 miles per hour slower than his fastball, he presses his middle finger against the seam and snaps his wrist upon release. This makes the ball spin fast; higher seams create a bigger ridge and make it easier to press harder. Although air resistance helps increase the movement, it's the

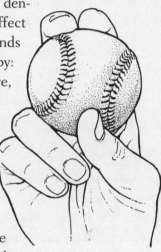

faster spin that makes the pitch nearly unhittable. One variation is the *knuckle-curve,* thrown with the tip of the index finger on the ball. The rest of the grip stays the same, and the pitch moves like a normal curve, but it feels more comfortable to some guys. When a right-handed batter faces a right-handed pitcher (or when a lefty faces a lefty), a curveball initially looks like it's speeding right at his head, causing him to flinch before the pitch bends away from him for a strike. That's why hitters prefer to face pitchers who throw with the opposite hand.

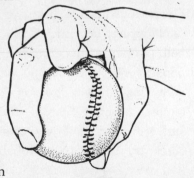

SLIDER (aka *biter, slide piece*)—Similar to a cutter but thrown a bit slower, a slider is like a fast curveball with more lateral movement. The pitcher presses his middle finger against the seam—as he does when throwing a curve—to create the tightest spin possible. There are three variations:

- A *backdoor* slider starts outside and breaks over the plate at the last second.

- A *backup* slider stays over the inside part of the plate.

- A *slurve*[1] combines the movement of a slider and a curve.

CHANGE-UP (aka *dead fish, palmball, change-of-pace, fosh*)— Named because of its change in velocity, the change-up makes the hitter swing too soon because the pitcher throws it with the same arm speed as his fastball, but gets it to travel about 10 miles per hour slower by holding the ball with his entire palm. The most popular change-up, a *circle-change,* is gripped with the tips of the thumb and index finger touching to form a circle against one side of the ball, the pinkie squeezing the opposite side, and the middle and ring fingers grazing— almost hovering above—the surface. (Next time you play catch, try this grip. You probably

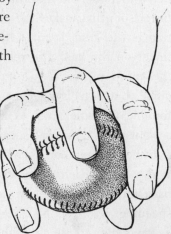

---

[1]Although some pitchers do throw a legitimate slurve, some announcers use the word just to cover their asses when they can't tell the difference.

won't get a 10-mph differential, but you'll notice that you can't throw quite as fast.)

SPLIT-FINGER FASTBALL (aka *splitter, splitty, forkball*)—This could be in the fastball section, but it's a specialty pitch with unique movement. Every pitcher throws a fastball; not every pitcher throws a splitter. Gripped with the index and middle fingers spread far apart, this pitch travels almost as fast as a fastball and drops as it reaches the plate. Because the ball is literally wedged between the fingers, the pitcher's arm ligaments get stretched and separated—but hey, it's worth it because many hitters end up chasing pitches out of the strike zone. A forkball is a slower version that drops even more because of its wider and deeper grip.

KNUCKLEBALL (aka *knuckler, floater, dancer, flutterball, rabbit, butterfly, moth*)—Thrown only 50 to 70 mph, this is by far the weirdest and most difficult pitch to throw, hit, and catch. Guess what: there are no knuckles involved. Instead, the pitcher presses his fingernails into the surface and, upon release, pushes the ball with his fingertips in order to throw it with no spin. This allows the seams to pick up air resistance, causing the ball to flutter (or "knuckle") unpredictably, like a Wiffle ball with a pebble stuck in the middle. A knuckleballer never begins his career as a knuckleballer—he develops this trick pitch as a last resort when all else fails. The pitch is so tricky that he can throw it more than 90 percent of the time; even though the hitter knows what's coming, he can't hit it.[2] Even though the catcher knows what's coming and wears an oversized mitt, he still struggles to catch it. And it's so tough to throw that there are usually just a couple of knuckleballers in the majors at any given time.

SCREWBALL (aka *scroogie, fadeaway*)— This obsolete pitch screws up the pitcher's arm more than it screws up the batter because it requires an exceptionally unnatural motion upon release. When throwing a curve, a righty pitcher snaps his wrist from right to left; on a screwball, his snap goes from left to right, causing the pitch to dart inside to a right-handed batter. Want to get an idea of how hard it is to throw? Try turning a doorknob the wrong way and imagine throwing the ball 75 mph at the same time.

SPITBALL (aka *shineball*)—The pitcher applies saliva (or another slippery substance, like Vaseline) to his fingers so he can squeeze and squirt the ball out of his hand. Moving like a fast knuckleball, this pitch is erratic, dangerous, and so unfair

---

[2]Almost every batter hates this mysterious pitch because it can easily throw off his timing and send him into a *slump*. Some *switch-hitters* think they can avoid this by batting right-handed against right-handed knuckleballers. Is this the answer? Even Charlie Lau, the most famous hitting coach ever, wasn't sure. "There are two theories on hitting the knuckleball," he said. "Unfortunately, neither of them works."

that it was ruled illegal, along with other doctored pitches like the mudball and *emeryball,* before the 1921 season—but Major League Baseball officials allowed the 17 pitchers who depended on the pitch before it was banned to continue to use it for the remainder of their careers. Hall of Famer Burleigh Grimes threw the last legal spitball in 1934.

EEPHUS[3] (aka *blooper, dewdrop, folly floater, LaLob*)—You know how a slow-pitch softball pitcher lobs the ball way up in the air toward home plate? That's what an eephus looks like. Even though it's often tossed more as a joke than as an *out-pitch,* it's still hard to hit because the ball passes through the strike zone at an unusually sharp angle. Not only will the batter struggle to make solid contact, but he might become overanxious and lose his timing. There are several active pitchers who throw high-arcing curveballs in the 50-mph range, but a true eephus is so rare that you might never see one.

GYROBALL—You're even less likely to see this pitch because it might not exist. It's baseball's version of Bigfoot; no one's really sure what to think. Two Japanese scientists used a supercomputer to invent the model for the gyroball, and just a handful of pitchers in the world are believed to be experimenting with it. Part screwball and part slurve, this mysterious pitch has been billed "unhittable" because of the unique arm angle and release, which combine to spin the ball in such a way that no batter has ever seen: like a spiraling

---

[3]"Eephus" is a nonsense word made up by Pirates outfielder Maurice Van Robays in the early 1940s. His teammate Rip Sewell invented the pitch after part of his foot was shot off in a hunting accident.

football in reverse (if thrown by a righty). While a fastball has backspin and a curve topples forward, the gyro—in theory—features a nearly undetectable counterclockwise sidespin that gives the pitch unprecedented movement.

The average pitcher uses just three or four different pitches (there's no way that one guy could master them all), but that's enough to keep the hitter guessing—unless the pitcher accidentally reveals what's coming. He might subconsciously fidget with the grip before firing his splitter, rush his *delivery* before throwing the circle-change, grunt when bringing the four-seamer, or stick out his tongue as he snaps off a curve. He might use different release points for each of his pitches or stand on different ends of the *rubber* to get certain angles on them. While the other team tries to identify the pitches, he makes sure he's not giving them away.

SIGNS

Just as the hitter gets fooled, the same would be true for the catcher if he didn't know what pitches to expect. He'd allow many more *passed balls* because the unpredictable movement of the pitches would make them difficult to catch. To prevent this, he decides which pitch should be thrown and communicates with his pitcher by giving signs with his bare hand, which he buries deep between his legs while crouching behind home plate.

Because the hitting team tries to steal the signs, the catcher must give them discreetly. He keeps his legs closed to prevent runners and coaches at first and third base from seeing his hand, which he holds high enough so his fingers aren't visible below his thighs. He also keeps an eye on the hitter to

make sure he doesn't peek backward. The hitter rarely does—
he knows that if he were to get caught, he'd get a little
chin music on the next pitch—but he can use his peripheral
vision to see when the catcher shifts toward one side of
the plate. Sometimes the angle of the sun or the position
of the stadium's lights casts a shadow of the catcher's crouch
in the hitter's direction. This means that if the catcher sets up
too soon, he reveals the intended pitch location, so he waits
until the last second. But if he waits too long, his moving target could distract the pitcher. A sneaky catcher might lean in
and smack his glove to make the hitter think he's setting up
inside, then shift quickly to the outside corner.

When you see the pitcher glaring toward the plate, he's not
trying to intimidate the hitter by looking mean. He's just
getting the signs. If you're lucky, you'll see a close-up of the
catcher flashing them. (Sometimes the catcher rubs his hand
in the chalk or puts white tape around his fingers or even
paints his fingernails with Wite-Out to make it easier for the
pitcher to see them.) It's fun to know what pitch is coming,
but unfortunately, the cameras are more likely to show you a
cute kid in the first row or the manager picking his nose.
Still, even long-distance shots would make it too easy for
teams to steal—and then relay—each other's signs, so televi-
sions are not allowed in the dugouts or bullpens.

Okay, so what are the actual signs? Usually, the catcher
flashes one finger for a fastball, two for a curve, and three for
other *breaking balls,* like sliders or splitters. He calls for a
change-up by showing or fluttering four fingers. He clenches
his fist for a *pitchout* and sticks out his thumb when the
pitcher should make a *pick-off* throw. If he wants the pitch
inside or outside, he pats the inside of one of his thighs or
points with his index or pinkie finger toward one side of the

plate. To request the height of the pitch, he might face his open palm toward the ground or sky.

Everything gets more complicated with a runner on second base because he can see the signs. Therefore, the *battery* uses a sequence of both real and phony signs to deceive him— otherwise, he'd relay them to the hitter. How? He could stand with his hands on his knees to indicate that a fastball is coming. He could make a fist to indicate location. Or he could adjust the sleeves on his jersey. Or touch his helmet or belt buckle. Or kick the dirt. Or clap.

Unfortunately, the pitcher and catcher sometimes confuse themselves instead of the runner. When the pitcher isn't sure what he's supposed to throw, he requests the signs again. If the catcher gets *crossed up,* possibly getting *handcuffed* by a fastball or failing to drop to his knees in time to block a breaking ball in the dirt, he'll head to the mound to review the signs—and when he does, he'll leave his mask on or hold his glove in front of his face to prevent the other team from reading his lips.[4] Then he might explain that the *third* series of signs he flashes, not the second, is the one in effect, and that if he swipes the dirt with his right hand, it means he's going to start over. And if he throws the ball back to the mound from his crouch, it means he wants the same pitch again no matter what signs he gives. And don't miss inside to this batter because he likes the ball in. And hurry up because I'm meeting a girl at the hotel bar at 11 and I plan on taking a shower beforehand. But don't stress out because you still have a three-run lead. And so on.

---

[4]In Game 1 of the 1989 NLCS, Giants first baseman Will Clark watched Cubs pitcher Greg Maddux during a conference on the mound and saw him mouth the words "fastball in" to manager Don Zimmer. On the next pitch, Clark hit a *grand slam.*

While the pitcher and catcher battle the hitter and runner, the *middle infielders* also look for the signs. They join conferences on the mound to stay informed because when they know what pitch is coming, they can *shade* or simply shift their weight in anticipation of the batter's lateness on a fastball or early swing on an *off-speed pitch*. They can also relay the signs to the outfielders. Baseball is a game of inches and fractions of seconds; getting an extra step or an explosive *jump* on the ball makes the difference between run-scoring hits and game-saving catches.

Fans start booing as a conference drags on, especially if the visiting team causes the delay. Sure, it gets annoying after a while, but it truly is part of the game, as is the umpire's trip to the mound to break it up. The next time someone whines that baseball doesn't have enough action, you can do two things: first, explain the planning, strategizing, calculating, and deception that take place before every pitch. Then quote Hall-of-Fame announcer Red Barber: "Baseball is dull only to dull minds."

PITCH SEQUENCE

High school and college coaches often decide what pitches are thrown. You can't blame them. They want to win, and they know more strategy than their teenage catchers. But this doesn't give kids a chance to learn from their mistakes. Amateur coaches unintentionally thwart player development, and many catchers enter professional baseball having never called their own games.

Even a major league catcher might not choose the pitches in crucial situations. When you see him stare off to one side before facing the pitcher and giving the signs, he's looking into his dugout where the manager or pitching coach tells him what to call. Obviously, the coach can't flash one or two or three fingers because the other team is watching him, so he uses a separate system of signs that only his catcher knows. (The coaching staff also calls some of the pickoffs and most pitchouts.) If the coach chooses the pitches, the pitcher does what he's told. But when the catcher calls his own game, the pitcher can *shake off* the signs. He might disagree with the selection or location or simply have more confidence throwing a different pitch.

When suggesting a pitch, the catcher usually starts with the fastball. Knowing this, the hitter looks for something off-speed when he sees the pitcher shake his head. Knowing that the hitter knows this, the pitcher might shake off a nonexistent sign to trick him into thinking that the fastball isn't coming when, in fact, it's on the way. And sometimes, instead of shaking his head, the pitcher simply looks at the catcher until he sees a sign that he likes. This type of deception can help the pitcher, even when he's *behind in the count,* by creating slight uncertainty for the hitter.

Every pitch should accomplish something. Even a *waste-pitch* on 0-2 (no balls, two strikes) should be close enough to the strike zone to make the hitter think about swinging. The same is true of a *purpose-pitch.* That's what you call a high and inside fastball designed to intimidate the hitter and leave him less likely to dive aggressively into the next pitch. With two strikes, the pitcher can then exploit the batter's fear by aiming low and away with a breaking ball. If he throws it perfectly, only an exceptionally disciplined hitter would be able to let it go. Anyone else would be lucky to hit a foul ball.

Watch how the pitcher and catcher avoid falling into a pattern with their pitch sequence. Some batters get a fastball on the first pitch. Others get something off-speed. Notice how the pitcher moves the ball inside and outside, up and down. Think about what he and his catcher are building toward. See if you can predict some of the pitches.

LOCATION, LOCATION, LOCATION

The only time the pitcher intentionally *grooves the ball* is when he's behind in the count and absolutely needs a strike. Normally, he tries to throw every pitch to a specific location within the strike zone. But even when he misses the zone, don't assume it was an accident. When he's *ahead in the count* or facing a *free-swinger,* he aims just off the plate—or a little high, or a little low—to get the batter to *go fishing.*

In addition to trying to guess the type of pitch, the hitter thinks about location. Sometimes he can predict both based on the situation or on how the defense is positioned:

- With a runner on first base and less than two outs, the pitcher wants to get the hitter to ground into a *double play.* Since a ground ball is usually hit on a low pitch—the result of the bat hitting the top half of the ball—the hitter anticipates pitches with downward movement, like curveballs, sinkers, and splitters.

- When the wind is blowing in, the batter knows that most fly balls will die before they leave the yard, so he prepares for high fastballs, which would cause him to swing underneath the ball and hit in the air.

- If the fielders are shading toward the *opposite field*—left field for a left-handed batter or right field for a righty—the hitter suspects that the pitcher will attack the *outer half* with fastballs to make him swing late and hit the ball in their direction.

- With a speedy runner on first, the catcher needs as much time as possible to throw the guy out if he steals, so the hitter looks for fastballs, which reach the catcher quicker than other pitches.

If you want to know where the pitcher will try to throw the ball, watch the catcher. Right before every pitch, he shifts his crouch and gives a target either on the inside or outside corner. Most pitchers hit the target most of the time. The best pitchers rarely miss, and even when they do, they often get away with it because they have such good *stuff*. Guys who are wild within the strike zone or who struggle just to find the zone don't stay in the Major Leagues very long.

In the majors, hitters generally get one good pitch to hit per at-bat—if they even get one. When you see a hitter get unusually frustrated after hitting a foul ball, it's because he wasted a rare opportunity, such as a *hanging curveball* or a four-seamer that caught too much of the plate. Of course, hitters still get cheap hits on great pitches while pitchers get away with mistakes, but most hard-hit balls occur when the pitcher falls behind in the count or misses his target.

THE COUNT

Even though a fastball seems like it would be the toughest pitch to hit—it's called "fast" for a reason—it's incredibly easy for the batter to connect with one when he knows it's coming. With a 2-0 count, he *sits dead red* because he knows that the pitcher needs to throw a strike to avoid falling further behind. That's why most players have better batting averages with the *bases loaded*; they know that the pitcher doesn't want to walk in a run, so his fastball becomes more predictable.

When the batter falls behind in the count, he has no idea what to expect. If he guesses, he might be wrong. If he doesn't guess and simply tries to react to the pitch once it's on the way, he'll be more likely to swing defensively and hit the ball weakly. Therefore, the pitcher's most important pitch is the first of the at-bat because it instantly determines who has the advantage. With a 1-0 count, the typical batter's average increases roughly 75 points. On 0-1, it drops by the same margin.

The pitcher holds a huge advantage on 0-2 because he doesn't need to throw a strike. (Some managers actually fine their pitchers for throwing 0-2 strikes.) He can try to *expand the strike zone* by aiming just outside of it, knowing that he'll still be in great shape at 1-2 if the batter doesn't swing.

"BALK!"

Sometimes the pitcher stops his delivery midmotion if he loses his footing or swallows his tobacco. With the bases empty, there's no penalty, but with *ducks on the pond*, it's considered one of many illegal attempts to deceive the base runner. Some of these illegal moves are subtle and unintentional, but if an umpire sees one, he'll throw his arms up, yell, "Balk!" and allow all runners to advance one base.

Here are some other rules that the pitcher must follow to avoid being charged with this costly infraction:

- He must be touching the rubber when he gets the catcher's sign and when he begins his delivery.

- He can't touch the rubber if he doesn't have the ball. (If he could, the runner wouldn't be able to guard against

the *hidden ball trick,* a rare defensive play on which an infielder secretly keeps the ball after a pick-off throw or a conference on the mound so he can *tag* out the runner as soon as he takes his lead.)

- When he's touching the rubber, he can't drop the ball.

- When he's pitching from the *stretch,* he must bring his bare hand and glove hand together in front of his body and hold them still for at least a split second before making his delivery. (This pause is called the *set,* short for the *set position,* and it prevents him from quick-pitching the runner.)

- When he's in the set, he can't separate his hands or move his shoulders.

- Before throwing to first base, a righty must lift his right foot and step off the back of the rubber. A lefty can do the same with his left foot, or he can simply lift his front leg and step toward first as he makes the throw.

- If a lefty's front foot crosses the back of the rubber on his leg kick, he must throw home unless he whirls and makes a pick-off throw to second base. If his front foot does not cross the rubber on the kick, he could throw home or to first base. (This keeps the runner near the base because he doesn't know where the pitcher will throw.) A righty can do the same thing when making a pick-off throw to third base. (See illustration on p. 30.)

- If the pitcher makes a pick-off throw while touching the rubber, he must step toward the base. (A lefty, for example, can't step toward home and throw to first. It's too sneaky.)

- He cannot fake a pick-off throw while touching the rubber, but with *runners on the corners*, a righty can step toward third and spin back toward first. (It hardly ever works. Fans always boo.)

- When he's on the mound, he can't touch his mouth with his bare hand, except on cold days when both managers agree and notify the umpires before the game that the pitchers should be allowed to blow on their hands. (This rule helps to prevent spitballs. If the pitcher violates it with the bases empty, the batter gets one ball added to the count.)

There are some legal moves the pitcher can use to deceive the runner, or at least limit his jump by keeping him closer to the base. A smart runner knows them all (and so will you after reading the baserunning chapter).

"OFF" DAYS

In December 1998, Kevin Brown became the first player to sign a contract worth more than $100 million when he agreed to pitch for the Dodgers for the next seven years. Although other players soon signed bigger contracts, Brown was still the highest-paid pitcher in 2003 when he earned $15,714,286. He appeared in 32 games that year, won 14 of them, and pitched 211 innings. That means he got paid over $1.1 million per win, over $491,000 every time he pitched a game (he didn't complete any), nearly $75,000 for each inning, and exactly $24,825.10 per out. Now, if you think that's bad, consider that Brown won a total of 14 games after he was traded to the Yankees for the final two years of his contract—and still didn't complete any games. (And if you think *that's* bad, then you must be forgetting the time he got particularly mad at himself after a poor outing in New York and picked a fight with a concrete wall in the clubhouse. The wall won.)

It's fun to break down the numbers, but it's not that simple when you consider what pitchers do on their off days, such as throwing, running, lifting weights, charting pitches, studying videotape, and chasing loose balls during batting practice.

CHARTS AND VIDEOTAPE

Each game, one of the unused starting pitchers keeps a chart of every pitch—movement, location, and results—thrown by his teammates. Usually, the guy who's scheduled to start the next day handles this task, and you can spot him because he'll be the only player in the dugout with a clipboard. Charting is tedious, but it's the best way for a team to recognize patterns of success and failure. For example:

- The team might notice that the bottom third of the opponent's lineup has trouble hitting off-speed pitches with two strikes.

- A pitcher could realize that his slider works better against righties.

- If the charts show that a certain hitter crushes inside fastballs to deep left-center, the pitcher can take advantage of his tendency and throw the ball inside if the ballpark has a deep fence on that side of the field. Or he can avoid pitching him *middle-in* if a strong wind is blowing in that direction.

In addition to studying charts, every pitcher reviews videotape of himself and his opponents. He analyzes his mechanics, learns the hitters' strengths and weaknesses, and assesses his own performance against them. Of course, the other team's hitters study videos too. (Some hitters have footage of all their at-bats on their video iPods.)

But charts and videos can't re-create the experience that players get by facing each other. Over the course of a decade (or just one season), the same pitchers and hitters square off so many times that they learn each other's tendencies the old-fashioned way. This gives the hitters the advantage. When a pitcher and hitter meet for the first time, the hitter has no idea what to expect because each pitcher has a unique rhythm, delivery, and release point. The pitcher, however, doesn't have as much to worry about because he knows that the batter swings hard all the time. In other words, there are more ways to throw a ball than to swing a bat. That's why rookie pitchers sometimes have a successful first month or two before struggling when they face teams for the second time, or why *starters* often begin games with several strong innings before getting knocked around during their second or third trips through the lineup. Of course, fatigue can also be a factor.

STAYING IN SHAPE

Relievers often pitch in back-to-back games, but starters can't; their arms would fall off without four days to recover, but they still do plenty of throwing during that time. They stay loose by playing catch, tighten their mechanics by working with the pitching coach, and build arm strength by *long-tossing,* a popular pregame exercise in which two guys play catch and gradually increase the distance until they're launching the ball several hundred feet. (The next time you go to a game, get there a couple hours early and you'll see them doing it.)

Nolan Ryan, who pitched a record 27 seasons and maintained his blazing fastball into his mid-40s, used to ride a stationary bike for hours after he pitched.[5] Leg strength is crucial for pitchers. It helps them push hard off the rubber and generate extra velocity. That's why running is a major part of every pitcher's exercise program.

[5]Other players have used extreme exercises and remedies to make themselves stronger. Roger Clemens, notorious for his strenuous workouts, used to grind his hand in a bucket of rice to strengthen his forearms and shoulders. Gregg Jefferies swung a lead bat underwater to strengthen his wrists. Jorge Posada, Moises Alou, and several other players admitted to urinating on their hands to toughen their skin ("Hi, nice to meet you"). Ryan treated his blisters with pickle juice.

GOING THE DISTANCE

In 1904 Jack Taylor pitched *complete games* in 39 consecutive starts. From 2001 to 2002, the Devil Rays played 194 consecutive games without a complete game. In 1908 Ed Reulbach pitched two complete-game *shutouts* in one day. In 2002 future Hall of Famer Pedro Martinez pitched two shutouts all season. In 1920 Leon Cadore and Joe Oeschger both pitched all 26 innings of a 1–1 tie. In 2003 Roy Halladay made headlines by lasting all 10 innings of a 1–0 victory because it was the first extra-inning complete-game shutout in 12 years.

What's going on here? Has the human body changed so much in the last century that it can't handle a few extra pitches? Even in the 1970s, some pitchers completed half their games and regularly threw 150 pitches per outing. That would be unheard of today, but no one thought much of it at the time because the decision to pull a pitcher from the game—practically an insult to one's manhood back then—was based entirely on performance.

Nowadays, coaches closely monitor their starters' pitch counts and yank them after 100 to 120 pitches. Only efficient pitchers have a chance to *go the distance*, while everyone else reaches the predetermined limit around the *seventh-inning stretch*—or they simply get tired because they're not trained to last longer. When pitchers lose energy, they lack the final oomph to push off from the rubber and finish strong. They can't quite get on top of the ball, so their pitches end up higher in the strike zone and are therefore easier to hit. This is especially true of curveballs, which require pitchers to reach extra high before snapping their wrists.

With a small lead late in the game, the manager sometimes *goes against the book* and sticks with his *ace*, whose momentum and passion could be more valuable than a bunch of charts and stats. But when the pitcher's determination can't overcome his loss of control and velocity, the manager uses his bullpen—and he sure has plenty of options:

- A *long reliever* takes over when the starter leaves the game after just a few innings.

- *Middle relievers* pitch an inning or two before the game reaches the final stretch.

- A *situational lefty* faces just one or two left-handed hitters.

- The *set-up man* preserves the lead in the eighth inning.

- The *closer* finishes the game in a *save* situation.

Some teams have such strong relief pitching that they treat games like six- or seven-inning contests. They feel that they're guaranteed to win when they reach the bullpen with a lead. But in baseball nothing's a guarantee, especially the bullpen, where things can easily go wrong because everyone, it seems, has issues. The long reliever might be one of those guys who need extra time to warm up. The middle reliever might have already pitched three days in a row. The situational lefty might be completely ineffective against righties. The set-up man might be distracted by some problem from his personal life. The closer might not feel comfortable when he enters a game with men already on base. The pitching coach has to keep track of all this stuff and help the manager select the right guy in each situation. When the decision is made, the pitching coach calls the bullpen coach on the dugout phone and tells him who should start getting loose.

But why do teams now rely on relief pitching? Haven't starting pitchers' bodies become healthier and stronger with all the fancy diets and elaborate workout regimens? The answer is simple: money. Teams are more concerned with the long-term future than the outcome of individual games. They think they'll get more out of their high-paid superstars by using them less and avoiding injury—and it's hard to blame them.

Pitchers don't mind their smaller workloads. To get credit for a win, a starter needs to pitch just five innings (four in a rain-shortened contest) and leave with a lead that his teammates maintain for the rest of the game. And then he doesn't have to play again for five days.

Not bad.

Or is it? Most fans don't care about good pitching because they're more entertained by seeing a bunch of home runs followed by their favorite closer padding his save total with a stress-free ninth inning. But this stuff happens regularly, and it has reduced the need for good fundamentals. Why should a team sacrifice an out with a *bunt* or attempt a risky *double steal* when most guys in the lineup can hit a three-run homer?

When you come home late and flip on the game and find a *pitchers' duel* in the fourth inning, don't automatically think, "Good, I didn't miss anything." These days, preventing runs is more impressive than scoring them.

WHAT DO THEY TALK ABOUT ON THE MOUND?

A coach never visits the mound to congratulate his pitcher (although White Sox manager Ozzie Guillen admitted that he sometimes makes the trip so his kids can see him on TV). He might give the guy advice, discuss strategy, or simply stall so a reliever has more time to get loose. You never really know, but here are some possibilities:

- **Mechanics**—"You're not pushing off with your back leg. You're leaving the fastball up, and your curve is flat."

- **The batter's strengths and weaknesses**—"This guy likes the ball in, so stay away unless you're sure you're gonna miss inside."

- **Pitch selection and sequence**—"He's sitting dead red on the first pitch and looking to lift the ball, so start him with something off-speed and keep everything down. If he doesn't bite, how do you feel about pitching to him behind in the count?"

- **Considering an intentional walk**—"You got the big man coming up with an *open base*. You wanna pitch to him or put him on and try to get the next guy to *roll one over*?"

- **Defensive strategy**—"Hold him on. If he takes off, we're gonna *throw through* and nail him."

- **Pep talk**—"Trust your fastball. You wouldn't be here if you didn't have good stuff."

- **Calming the pitcher after several cheap hits**—"You should be back in the dugout right now. Stay focused. Limit the damage. Let's get out of this."

- **Lighthearted distraction**—"Where are you eating after the game? I was craving a steak all day, but La Russa just told me about this delightful vegetarian place right across from the hotel."

- **Fatigue**—"How ya holdin' up? Can you get us through this inning?"

Although fatigue is a serious issue, it's not always handled in a serious manner. Mets pitcher Tug McGraw (the guy who coined the phrase "Ya gotta believe") once begged manager Casey Stengel to leave him in the game for one more batter. "I struck him out the last time I faced him," he said.

"Yeah," Stengel replied, "but the last time you faced him was this same inning."

Years later, Rangers reliever Jim Kern recalled a conversation with his manager who was about to pull him from the game. "I told him I wasn't tired. He told me, 'No, but the outfielders sure are.'"

TOMMY JOHN

Throwing overhand is an unnatural motion for the human body. Even though pitchers condition themselves to stay healthy, many of them still hurt their arms. Before recent advances in medicine, these injuries were often career-ending.

In 1974 a 31-year-old *junkballer* named Tommy John blew out his left elbow—in fancy terms, he tore his ulnar collateral ligament. Knowing his career was over unless he tried something radical, he and a doctor named Frank Jobe attempted the first ligament replacement surgery. Given a 1-in-100 chance of recovery, John amazed both the medical and baseball worlds simply by returning to the Major Leagues. Then he pitched 14 more seasons and won an additional 164 games.

In this operation, which has since saved countless careers and been named *Tommy John surgery,* the surgeon removes the damaged elbow ligament and replaces it with an otherwise unneeded tendon from the wrist, hand, forearm, or occasionally the leg or toe. Pitchers now have a 90 percent chance of making a full recovery with a year of rehabilitation. (Some pitchers return throwing harder than they did before the operation, but that wasn't the case for John. "When they operated on my arm," he said, "I asked them to put in a Koufax fastball. They did, but it turned out to be Mrs. Koufax.")

Dr. Lewis Yocum and Dr. James Andrews are now the leading specialists in performing the surgery. Many big-name pitchers have successfully undergone the one-hour operation, including John Smoltz, Kerry Wood, Jason Isringhausen, Mariano Rivera, John Franco, Eric Gagne, Bob Wickman, Kris Benson, Matt Morris, and David Wells, who holds the record for most wins after Tommy John surgery. Doctors now believe that the procedure could have extended the career of Hall of Famer Sandy Koufax, whose arm problems forced him to retire abruptly in his prime.

THE CY YOUNG AWARD

Denton True Young was called "Cy" because he whirled and pitched so fast that he looked like a cyclone. When his legendary 22-year career ended in 1911, he had won 511 games and amassed many other extraordinary statistics.

In 1956 Major League Baseball commissioner Ford Frick created the annual Cy Young Award to honor the best pitcher in baseball. Selected by the Baseball Writers' Association of America (BBWAA), Don Newcombe of the NL's Brooklyn Dodgers was the first recipient, and starting in 1967, the award went to one pitcher in each league.

In 1974 Mike Marshall became the first reliever to win the award. Fernando Valenzuela (1981) remains the only rookie to win it, and Eric Gagne (2003) is the only pitcher with a losing record to claim the honor.[6] Greg Maddux and Randy

[6]Gagne went just 2–3 as the Dodgers' closer, but he had a 1.20 *earned run average* (ERA) and set a record by saving 55 games in 55 chances, so we forgive him.

Johnson each won four consecutive Cy Young Awards, and Roger Clemens holds the career record with seven.

Baseball historians have used early statistics and other factors to determine which players would have won awards if the awards had been around sooner. They say Cy Young would have won three Cy Young Awards.

CHAPTER 3
HITTING

The pitcher has got only a ball. I've got a bat. So the percentage of weapons is in my favor and I let the fellow with the ball do the fretting.

—Hank Aaron, all-time home run leader

THE LINEUP

Over the course of a season, the first few hitters in the lineup come to bat about 100 times more than those at the end. Think about it. If the fifth hitter makes the last out of the game, the sixth-through-ninth hitters each finish with one less *plate appearance* than everyone else. That's why better players hit first, but the manager doesn't arrange his lineup strictly from best to worst. If the strongest hitter batted first, many of his blasts would be wasted as *solo home runs*. If the fastest guy batted in the middle of the lineup, he wouldn't be able to steal as many bases because there'd be slower runners in front of him. Therefore, the manager carefully fills each slot with the player whose unique skills fit the situation he's likely to face. In addition, the manager avoids placing several righties or lefties consecutively to prevent one relief pitcher from comfortably facing all of them.

The *leadoff hitter* is the offensive igniter. His job is to get on base and use his speed to make something happen. But first he needs to be patient and *work the count*. Here's why:

- By *taking a pitch* or two, he and his teammates can watch the pitcher and get an idea of his style.

- On-base percentage is his most important statistic; the more pitches he sees, the better his chances of earning a walk.

- Going deep in the count gets the starter out of the game sooner by raising his pitch count.

The leadoff hitter has another important, yet underappreciated, duty. After the pitcher bats (pitchers almost always bat last) and makes an out, the leadoff man paces slowly toward the plate to give him extra time to walk back to the dugout. Pitchers are fragile. They should never exert themselves unless they're pitching.

The number-two hitter helps the leadoff man advance to *scoring position*. He needs to be a *contact hitter* with excellent bat control, not only to protect the runner on the *hit-and-run* play, but to be able to hit with two strikes after taking a few pitches to give his speedy teammate a chance to steal second base. Sometimes he bunts. Other times he *hits behind the runner*—all this while trying to get on base.

The best hitter on the team usually bats third. His power drives in runs, and his ability to reach base in front of the *cleanup hitter* helps him score.

The player most likely to hit a homer bats fourth because he often comes up with runners on base. This is the ideal slot in the batting order, except for one possibility: when he strides to the *on-deck circle* with two outs in the first inning, he doesn't know if he'll get a chance to bat. He still prepares in case the number-three hitter reaches base, but when a *one-two-three inning* wipes out his turn, he has to regain his adrenaline at the beginning of the next *frame*.

If you were a pitcher and had to face the best hitter on the team, but saw a lousy player in the on-deck circle, what would you do? You'd intentionally walk the All-Star and challenge the chump. That's why the number-five hitter is important. He has to be good enough that his mere presence in the lineup forces the pitcher to throw strikes to the batter in front of him.

Ideally, the sixth and seventh batters have enough skill to knock in a few runs, but don't expect much from the bottom of the order. In the National League, the eighth hitter is the worst-hitting position player on the team, but he still plays an important role: by reaching base with two outs, he *clears the pitcher's slot*. In other words, he allows the pitcher to come to bat and get his turn over with so his team can start the next inning with the top of the order.

Pitching and hitting require such different skills that one person is rarely talented enough to succeed at both and rarely has time to practice both. Sure, pitchers take their cuts during early *BP* to get loose and to remember what a bat feels like, but they don't do much beyond that. That's why they're such bad hitters.

Despite their lousy hitting, some pitchers bat over .200 and help their own cause by driving in the occasional run. With less than two outs and a runner on base, they attempt to *sacrifice bunt*. Otherwise, they swing hard in case they hit it.

The all-time record for the most at-bats in a season without a hit belongs to a pitcher, of course. Bob Buhl began his historic drought after being traded to the Cubs early in the 1962 season. He finished 0-for-70 and struck out in more than half his at-bats. But hey, at least he was consistent.

THE ON-DECK CIRCLE

The hitter awaiting his turn gets his muscles loose in the on-deck circle by swinging a weighted bat. This makes his bat feel lighter when he steps to the plate and increases his *bat speed* (or at least boosts his confidence by making him think he's swinging faster), allowing him to wait longer before *pulling the trigger.*

Hitters do other things in the on-deck circle beyond loosening up. Many guys rub *pine tar*[1] on their bats, others try to establish their timing with full swings, and some simply kneel and watch the pitcher. Occasionally, you'll see the on-deck hitter stray toward the area behind the plate to get a better look—but if he strays too far and gets in the pitcher's line of vision, the ump will order him back.

FUNDAMENTALS

"Wait for your pitch. Okay now, keep your eye on the ball . . . ready to swing level? And . . . follow through!"

Nag, nag, nag.

[1] On July 24, 1983, the famous "pine tar incident" occurred at Yankee Stadium. After Royals third baseman George Brett hit a two-run homer in the ninth inning to give his team a 5–4 lead, Yankees manager Billy Martin complained to home-plate umpire Tim McClelland that Brett's pine tar exceeded the legal limit of 18 inches from the tip of the handle. McClelland inspected the bat and ruled Brett out, sparking a protest from the Royals and a nationwide uproar. American League president Lee McPhail eventually overruled McClelland and reinstated Brett's homer. The rest of the game was played 25 days later, and the Royals held on for a 5–4 win. Why can't a player cover his whole bat with pine tar? Would it make the ball go farther? No, but the fielders would have to handle a gooey ball, and that wouldn't be fair. (Watch for batters who love the sticky stuff so much that they keep a stash on their helmets.)

Parents and coaches say it so often that it gets annoying. But they're right. Even major leaguers struggle when they overlook these obvious tips.

There are so many other fundamentals that a hitter would go crazy if he tried to remember them all before each pitch. That's why he hits off a batting tee, does *soft-toss,* and takes BP both on the field and in underground batting cages; he works hard to build muscle memory so his instincts will take over and guide him through these basics:

STANCE The batter can see the ball better with an open stance because his head and eyes face more toward the pitcher, whereas a closed stance prevents his body from flying open too soon. (When that happens, he loses power and jerks his head— not a good way to keep his eye on the ball.) *Plate coverage* is essential: he stands close enough to reach the outside corner, but far enough away to extend his arms without getting jammed on an inside strike. He might reach out with his bat and tap the far edge of the plate to measure his distance from it.

GRIP Have you noticed that some home run swings almost look effortless? That's because the hitter avoids squeezing the bat tight enough to make sawdust sprinkle to the ground. He stays relaxed and lines up his knuckles—not the biggest knuckles, but the ones he uses to knock on a door.

WEIGHT SHIFT Big muscles might look nice, but the batter generates most of his power by shifting his weight. He starts with roughly 60 percent of it on his back leg and leans back even farther before the pitcher delivers. Then he steps forward to attack the ball. Whether he uses a huge leg kick or barely lifts his front foot, he tries to keep his hands back until the last second so he can still make solid contact if he gets fooled by an off-speed pitch and strides early.

SWING A level swing is more likely to produce a line drive, so the batter keeps his hands and back elbow up; if he lowers them, he might *uppercut* and loft a lazy fly ball. He hits with more power by *pulling the ball,* but if he pulls an outside pitch, he'll probably break his bat or ground weakly to a middle infielder. Similarly, it's tough to hit an inside pitch to the opposite field, though certain situations call for it. In general, he should simply go with what the pitcher gives him.

FOLLOW-THROUGH Before the 1970s, hitting coaches instructed their players to keep both hands on the bat when following through. Then Charlie Lau came along. He was the first coach to encourage his guys to take one hand off. Everyone thought he was crazy, but his method worked. To this day, no one's sure whether one- or two-handed follow-throughs work better, so batters decide for themselves.

When Ted Williams, perhaps the greatest hitter of all time, said that "hitting is 50 percent above the shoulders," he meant that a solid mental approach helps as much as proper physical mechanics. The batter shouldn't admire his picture on the JumboTron or glance at the pretty women in the front row, nor should he worry if his back pocket is turned inside out or brood about the *official scorer* who gave him an error when the ball really took a *bad hop*. He must stay focused and confident and overcome the fear of failing; the best hitters succeed merely three times out of ten.

And of course he should keep his eye on the ball.

BUNTING

Swinging as hard as possible is not always the best idea. In certain situations, the batter can take advantage of the infielders' deep positioning by holding his bat over home plate and gently bunting the ball.

Easy, right?

Not always. In addition to popping up or striking out by bunting foul with two strikes, the maneuver can be dangerous. Players occasionally break their fingers while trying to *lay one down* because they don't hold the bat properly.

On a sacrifice bunt, the batter attempts to advance the runner without worrying about his own fate. Even though he's not trying to fool the defense, he shouldn't *square around* too soon and make his intention obvious. (The pitcher, knowing that the batter might square around on *first movement*, will often make a pick-off throw just to get him to reveal the play.) Here are some other bunting basics:

- He holds the bat *letter-high* to remind himself not to chase anything above his hands.

- He keeps the *barrel* above the handle to avoid popping up; to bunt a low pitch, he bends his knees and lowers his entire body rather than dropping the bat head.

- He holds the barrel with his thumb and index finger, keeping most of his hand behind the bat for protection. (See illustration on p. 49.)

- Instead of jabbing at the ball, he deadens it by absorbing the contact, almost as if catching it with the bat.

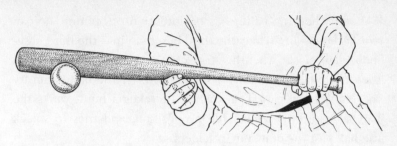

Some speedsters have better batting averages when they bunt than when they swing. This doesn't mean it's easy to bunt for a hit. It's always such a close play at first that the batter does everything possible to gain an extra fraction of a second:

- When facing a right-handed pitcher, the batter aims his bunt toward the third-base side because the momentum of the pitcher's follow-through takes him toward the first-base side of the mound.

- When bunting toward the third-base side, the batter tries to place the ball just inside the foul line. The closer he bunts toward it, the longer it takes the pitcher to get there. If he's going to miss, he'd rather miss foul than fair so he can return to the box with one strike instead of returning to the dugout after handing the pitcher an easy out.

- Bunting to the right side is riskier because the fielder has a short throw to first base. If the batter bunts in that direction, he either aims close to the foul line or tries to push the ball past the mound, bringing the first baseman out of position and forcing the pitcher or second baseman to cover the *bag*.

- A left-handed hitter starts moving toward first base before the pitch reaches him so that his momentum is already going in the right direction by the time he makes contact. This is called a *drag bunt*.

Even when the batter has no intention of bunting, he can *run his hands up* to draw the third baseman in—the third baseman plays closer when he suspects the hitter will bunt—and then try to slap the next pitch past him. Or the batter can try the *butcher-boy* play. That's when he fakes a bunt, yanks the bat back into his regular hitting position, and tries to smack the ball past the drawn-in infielders.

FUNNY STANCES

Some batters wiggle their butts before they get set in the box. Others stand funny, hold the bat funny, and step funny. But no matter how strange they look while waiting for the pitch, their hands and bodies always return to the same ready position before they swing. The extra movements are just timing mechanisms or silly habits.

SWITCH-HITTING

Some players are talented enough to bat from either side of the plate. This gives them a slight advantage no matter who is pitching. They're called switch-hitters, and ten of them have reached the Hall of Fame: Dave Bancroft, Cool Papa Bell, Max Carey, George Davis, Frankie Frisch, Biz Mackey, Mickey Mantle, Eddie Murray, Red Schoendienst, and Ozzie Smith. (Pete Rose also switch-hit.)

Of the players who switch-hit, many learned to do so as kids because their backyards and playgrounds were shaped in such a way that forced or rewarded them for hitting the ball to the opposite field. Rather than waiting on the pitches, they batted from the other side of the plate and tried to pull them. Other players learned to switch-hit from their coaches and fathers, who knew that their kids wouldn't get *platooned* later in their careers if they could hit from both sides.

Switch-hitters usually favor one side of the plate, often hitting for power one way and average the other. Many of them naturally hit right-handed but face so many righties that they become better hitters from the left side.

Here are two weird rules for you:

- The batter is allowed to switch to the other side of the plate during his at-bat, except when there are two strikes.

- The pitcher is allowed to throw with either arm, but he can't switch during an at-bat.[2]

HITTING WITH TWO STRIKES

The average major leaguer bats under .200 with two strikes. While no one wants to fall behind in the count, a *power hitter* probably won't change his approach when he does. He's not up there simply to protect the plate and make contact; he gets paid to hit home runs, so he swings for the fences no matter what. (With this attitude, he'll also strike out once per game.)

---

[2]There have been four switch-pitchers in major league history, starting with Tony Mullane, who played from 1881 to 1894 and remains the only guy to pitch ambidextrously—in the same game—more than once. Greg A. Harris, a natural righty with a custom-made glove that fit either hand, became the last switch-pitcher when he threw left-handed to two batters during a scoreless inning of relief for the 1995 Montreal Expos. (The Expos moved to Washington, D.C., in 2005 and became the Nationals.)

A contact hitter, however, makes minor adjustments with two strikes, such as *choking up* to shorten his swing and gain better bat control.

Normally, the batter stands as far back in the box as possible, digging his back foot into the chalk line to blur the boundary and gain a few extra inches. (He can move anywhere within the box at any time, but if his foot is outside of it when he makes contact, he's automatically out.) The farther back he stands, the more time he has before the pitch reaches him. But because the pitcher throws more off-speed pitches with two strikes, the batter sometimes moves forward to prevent the ball from breaking before it gets to him. By moving forward, he also increases the angle within which he can hit a fair ball because he'll make contact in front of the plate.

RUN FACTORY

There are times when a team becomes so desperate to score that it sacrifices a few outs—and possibly a few runs—to make sure that one man crosses the plate. *Extra-base hit?* Forget about it. The team doesn't even need a single. All it takes is a base runner and simple fundamentals to *manufacture a run.* The leadoff man, for example, could get hit by a pitch, steal second, move to third on a groundout to the right side, and score on a *sacrifice fly.*

OUCH!

On August 16, 1920, Yankees right-hander Carl Mays threw a pitch that hit Indians shortstop Ray Chapman on the head. Chapman died the next day and is still the only major leaguer who died from an on-field injury. Although Mays was a spit-baller, his fateful pitch might have been a fastball. No one's sure. But Chapman's death was the main reason spitballs were banned the following season.

It wasn't until 1941 that the New York Giants became the first team to wear batting helmets. Thirty years later, helmets were mandatory for everyone, and the single earflap became a required addition in 1982.

Nowadays, image is everything. When a guy gets *plunked*, he'll strut to first base like nothing happened. He won't wince. He won't grimace. He won't get an ice pack. He won't cry. He won't even rub it. That wouldn't be manly.

But how much does it *really* hurt? Consider the speed of the pitch and how it hit him. Was it a 93-mph fastball? A 77-mph curve? A 64-mph knuckleball? Did the ball nick him and hardly change direction? Did it plow right into him and drop to the dirt? What body part did it hit? A meaty shoulder or thigh? A bony wrist or elbow? Occasionally, a fastball will break the batter's hand and sideline him for weeks or months.

Machismo aside, almost every pitch that meets flesh leaves a bruise, and if the batter is in serious pain, he'll get a visit from the trainer.

BROKEN AND FLYING BATS

Why does everyone love the "crack" of the bat? A cracking noise means the bat broke. Listen carefully and you can distinguish this jarring noise from the delightful click that the bat produces when the hitter rips the ball off the *sweet spot*.

If a hitter suspects his bat is broken—a bat can crack and still appear intact—he holds the barrel and taps the knob on the ground. If it's broken, he'll feel it vibrate and possibly hear a pinging noise.

Every hitter feels comfortable with his *gamer*. If he loses his grip and sends it flying into the stands, he might trade a different bat to the lucky fan for the one that got away. (Stadium security conducts the transaction.)

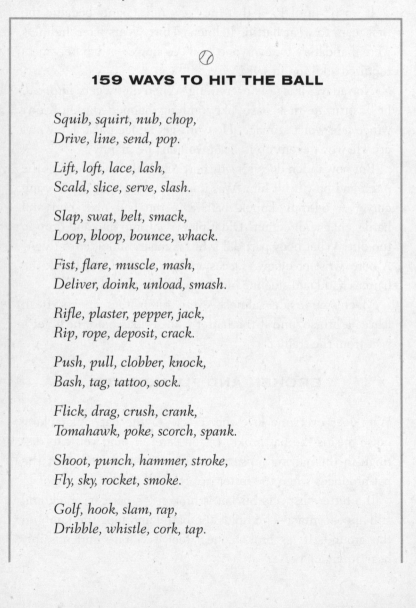

159 WAYS TO HIT THE BALL

Squib, squirt, nub, chop,
Drive, line, send, pop.

Lift, loft, lace, lash,
Scald, slice, serve, slash.

Slap, swat, belt, smack,
Loop, bloop, bounce, whack.

Fist, flare, muscle, mash,
Deliver, doink, unload, smash.

Rifle, plaster, pepper, jack,
Rip, rope, deposit, crack.

Push, pull, clobber, knock,
Bash, tag, tattoo, sock.

Flick, drag, crush, crank,
Tomahawk, poke, scorch, spank.

Shoot, punch, hammer, stroke,
Fly, sky, rocket, smoke.

Golf, hook, slam, rap,
Dribble, whistle, cork, tap.

Cream, juice, punish, drill,
Maul, whip, pummel, kill.

Shellac, ram, crunch, slip,
Strike, nick, powder, tip.

Roll, skip, inside-out,
Guide, place, blister, clout.

Uncork, nail, volley, rake,
Cue, foul, top, take.

Wallop, clock, sting, pound,
Paste, launch, tee, ground.

Elevate, zap, dink, club,
Skim, starch, wattle, drub.

Jerk, jolt, hack, chip,
Thunder, lather, lambaste, clip.

Float, nudge, squeeze, squeak,
Buzz, tear, deaden, sneak.

Bang, blast, yank, dunk,
Flip, fight, slug, plunk.

Rock, scoop, hoist, drop,
Park, spray, power, plop.

Work, put, rattle, thump,
Curl, sizzle, bludgeon, dump.

CHAPTER 4
BASERUNNING

I know my face looks old, but if you slid head-first for 16 years, you'd be ugly too.

—Pete Rose, all-time hits leader

THE RULES

If you already know the difference between a force-out and a tag-out, you may be tempted to skip this section.

Don't.

Even a simple rule like this can get tricky, but before getting into it, let's take one minute to explain the difference to people who might have missed it. When a runner has to go to a certain base, it's called a *force play,* and he can be *retired*—a fancy way to say that he's put "out"—by a fielder who simply touches the base while holding the ball. Because two runners can't occupy the same base, a runner on first is forced to run to second on a grounder to make room for the batter; runners on first and second are both forced to run to second and third, and if the bases are loaded, there's a force at every base.

Here's where it starts to get a little hairy.

If the batter hits a grounder with runners on the corners, the man on first has to run to second, but the guy on third does not have to run home. That's because there's an open base behind him. If he decides to go for home, there's no force play, so he must be touched—or tagged—with the ball. (The ball can be in the fielder's glove, and although you won't see it too often, a runner can be tagged out on a force play.) There are lots of situations when there's no force, such as trying to stretch a single into a double, running home from second on a *base hit,* stealing a base, and racing from first to third on a sharp grounder through the right side. Even when the runner dives back to first base on a pick-off throw, there's no force. It might seem like he has to go back to first—certainly that's the smartest move—but if he wanted to, he could dart toward second instead.

Break out the razor. It's about to get even hairier.

Suppose there's a runner on first with less than two outs. If the first baseman fields a grounder and steps on the bag to retire the batter, first base becomes open, and the runner—now between bases—is no longer forced to go to second. Usually, however, he'll continue on his way, and when he does, the first baseman yells "Tag!" as he throws the ball so the shortstop knows there's no force.

Here are some more baserunning rules:

FLY BALLS When a batted ball is caught *on a fly* with less than two outs, the runner must return to his base. After it's caught—or touched if the fielder bobbles and then catches it—he can advance. (This is called *tagging up.*) If the runner takes off from first base and rounds second before realizing that a fly ball has been caught, he must retouch second base as he heads back toward first. Of course, if there are already two outs, he has no reason to wait or retreat because the inning will end as soon as the outfielder snags the ball.

THE BASELINE At some point you've probably heard that the runner isn't allowed to run out of the baseline. Well, guess what? This is true only if he strays more than three feet to avoid being tagged or blocks a throw to first base by running outside of the *runner's box*. He's actually required to leave the baseline to dodge a fielder who's attempting to catch a batted ball. If he touches the fielder, the ump will charge him with interference and call him (or the batter) out. But when there's no action in the baseline, the runner can wander off as far as he likes.

OVERSLIDING At second and third, the runner can be tagged out if he runs or slides past the base even after reaching it safely. He's allowed to run or slide past the plate, and he can do the same when running from home to first—his momentum can carry him all the way down the right-field line, and he can leisurely stroll back without being tagged as long as he doesn't turn toward second—but he can't overslide first when returning to it. Why slide at all? It helps the runner avoid being tagged, and it quickly reduces his momentum as he plows into the base, allowing him to run full speed until the last second.

TWO RUNNERS ON ONE BASE Let's say there are runners on second and third with less than two outs. The batter hits a shallow fly ball, and the runner on second thinks the ball won't be caught, so he starts running. The runner on third thinks it will be caught, so he waits to tag up. The ball drops for a hit, but it's too shallow for him to score, so he stays on third. The *trail runner* is now standing on third with him. Big trouble. Two runners, as you know, can't occupy the same base, but they're not automatically out. The runner who has not yet advanced to the next base (in this case, the guy who started on third) is allowed to stay there, so the defensive team needs to take action. Usually, the closest fielder frantically tags them both and waits for the umpire to make a call.

PASSING A RUNNER The runner is out if he runs past a teammate. The fielding team doesn't even need to tag him.

HIT BY A BATTED BALL If the runner gets hit in fair territory, he's out, and the batter gets credit for a hit. If the batter gets hit by his own batted ball outside the batter's box and in fair territory, he's out, but he doesn't get credit for a hit. If he did—and if he were selfishly playing for his own statistics, as many guys do—he could bunt down the first-base line, chase the ball, and kick it.

STRATEGIES

News flash for geometry teachers: the shortest distance between two points is not a straight line. Need proof? Watch how the batter runs from home to first after he pokes a base hit into the outfield, and you'll see that his path resembles the curved shape of a banana. This helps him round first base and take a more direct route toward second. More proof? When the runner *takes a lead* off second, he stands several steps behind the baseline so he can round third and head home—pretty basic but extremely important.

Here are some other baserunning strategies:

THREE BALLS, TWO STRIKES, TWO OUTS With two outs and a *full count,* the runner always takes off with the pitch to get a head start—unless there's an open base behind him. As long as there's a force, he can't be thrown out no matter what the batter does; a walk pushes him to the next base, a batted ball forces him to run, and a strikeout ends the inning.

GOING FOR THIRD The runner should take special care not to make the first or third out of an inning at third base. If he reaches second with no outs, he should play it safe because there's already a good chance he'll score. With one out, however, he should take a chance and try to make it to third. If he's successful, he'll be able to score on a groundout or a fly ball instead of relying on his teammates to drive him in from second with a base hit.

OUTFIELDERS In addition to reviewing videotapes and scouting reports of opposing hitters and pitchers, every team studies the opposing team's outfielders. Even if one of them has an exceptionally strong arm, the manager might encourage his runners to be aggressive and go for the extra base, putting pressure on the guy to make a perfect throw.

SAFETY Runners sometimes hold batting gloves in each hand to force themselves to make fists. This prevents their fingers from getting stepped on or jammed as they slide.

HOW TO SLIDE People argue whether the runner can reach a base as quickly with a foot-first slide as he can with a head-first dive. Supposedly, it makes no difference, but everyone agrees that using nature's padding with a foot-first slide is safer, especially at home plate, where the catcher stands well protected with *spikes,* shin guards, a helmet, and other equipment.

FANCY SLIDES The runner slides to one side of the base when a throw is coming in from the other. On a pick-off

throw to first, he dives for the outside corner because it's farther from the pitcher, but on a throw from left field to third
base, he slides to the inside edge, which is farther from the
outfielder. Fancy foot-first slides have their own names:

- *Hook slide*—The runner eludes the fielder by sliding past
  the base and snaring it with his back foot.

- *Pop-up slide*—The runner slides directly into the firmly
  planted base in order to push himself up in one motion.
  Then he can keep running if the ball gets loose.

- *Takeout slide*—The runner slides late and crashes into
  the fielder to prevent him from making another throw. It's
  legal as long as the runner stays within reach of the base.
  If he slides too far from it, the umpire can charge him
  with interference and call out the other runner too.
  (A takeout slide is the best way to legally get revenge
  after being hit by a pitch.)

WHEN NOT TO SLIDE There are two situations in which the runner should not slide. The first is when racing a throw that comes from directly behind him—for example, when scurrying back to third on a pick-off throw by the catcher. By remaining upright, the runner blocks the throwing lane; the catcher has no clear target, and the third baseman struggles to see the ball. The other situation is when a throw easily beats him to the plate—the only way to score is to crash into the catcher and knock the ball loose. (If a runner on first takes only a small lead, he doesn't need to dive on a pick-off attempt. As he scampers back, you might see him shield the side of his face with his right hand to protect himself against a wild throw.)

THINKING BEFORE RUNNING By considering the situation and eyeing the defensive alignment before the pitch, the runner can confidently make split-second decisions. If he's on first when the batter clouts a deep fly ball, he needs to know how many outs there are and if the ball has a chance of being caught. Should he take off right away? Should he retreat and tag up? Should he drift toward second so he can score if the ball falls for a hit? How far should he drift? Halfway? Three-quarters of the way? What's the score? What inning is it? Is his team desperate to scratch out one run? Who's *on deck?* The cleanup hitter? The pitcher?

PLAYING IT SAFE The runner should not get thrown out on a grounder when he's not forced to run. As a general rule, he stays on second base when the ball is hit in front of him (to the shortstop or third baseman) and takes off for third when it's hit behind him (*up the middle* or to the right side). When he's on third with the *infield in,* he can try to beat the throw to the plate by running as soon as the batter makes contact. Of course, if the pitcher fields the ball, it'll be an easy out no matter what kind of jump the runner gets—which means he still needs to play it safe, even when he's going for it.

PINCH-RUNNER A player who runs in place of another runner is called a pinch-runner. Any player who's taken out of a game cannot return, so the manager must wait for the right moment to make the switch. He doesn't necessarily want the new guy to steal a base. Usually, he just needs a faster runner who can score from first on a double, reach second quicker and break up a double play, or simply put more pressure on the defense in a key situation.

FAKING IT There are two reasons why the runner takes off as if he's stealing, but then stops after a few steps and returns to his base:

- He gets a bad jump or loses his footing and changes his mind because he knows he has no chance.

- He deliberately fakes it in order to draw the defense out of position; one of the fielders has to run and cover the base, opening a hole for the hitter to poke one through.

While the runner rattles the pitcher with his antics, he might be distracting the batter too. Therefore, he chooses his pitch wisely and often stays put when his teammate is ahead in the count.

STAYIN' ALIVE When the runner gets caught in a *rundown*, he tries to stay alive as long as possible, not only to escape it, but to give other runners time to advance.

FOUL LEAD At third base, the runner takes his lead in foul territory so that he won't be out if he gets hit with a batted ball. After each pitch, he returns to the base in fair territory to block the catcher's throwing lane.

SIGNS

You might not notice it at the ballpark, but when you watch a game on TV and the batter looks off to the right side of the screen between pitches, he's getting the sign from his third-base coach. Bunt? Hit-and-run? Take a pitch? *Green light?* Stolen base? *Squeeze play?* Nothing?

It's possible.

The coach might be making nonsense gestures. If he tricks the other manager into shuffling his defense or calling a pitchout to defend against a potential steal, the batter gains a slight advantage.

Assuming the signs are real, what does it mean when the coach touches his nose, ear, nose again, and chin? How about when he swipes his left arm, right arm twice, forehead, chest, thigh, belt, the bill of his cap, and then claps three times? If you could figure it out, 29 other teams would gladly hire you as a spy. Generally, though, there's an *indicator*—one or more gestures or body parts or articles of clothing that validate or nullify everything else. Signs are simple in Little League. If a coach uses his cap as the indicator and his belt to mean "bunt," the batter bunts only if he sees the coach touch his belt directly after his cap. But things get much more complicated in the bigs, where a coach might use a cloth-to-skin sequence as the indicator, after which the actual sign might be the fourth gesture to follow, unless, for example, he cancels it by wiping his left rib cage an even number of times while looking at his shoes. Or if he flashes a certain sign before the first pitch of an at-bat and then puts a hold on it, the batter—or runner—knows he'll soon be executing the play and simply looks for the hold to be removed amid the dozens of phony signs that will follow.

The third-base coach also helps the runners by using various gestures:

- When he lifts both arms with open palms, it means, "Go to the base without sliding."

- When he holds one arm up and points at the base with the other, it means, "Don't slide, but stop directly on the base without overrunning it."

- When he flings both arms and hands toward the ground, it means, "Slide!"

- When he frantically swings one arm in a windmill motion, it means, "Keep running!" (While the coach is tempted to get close to the action to give his sign, he must take special care to stay out of the way; if the runner rounds third and bumps into him—or makes even the slightest contact—the player is automatically out.)

Occasionally, the coach gives two different instructions simultaneously if two runners need help. Why does a runner need help? Because he can't always see the ball. When the batter cranks an extra-base hit into the right-field corner, his back is to the ball as he approaches second base. By looking at his coach, he knows whether to stop there or try to stretch his hit into a triple—and whether he should slide.

Sometimes a runner will get help from his teammates.

When he can't tell how far a pitch has scooted from the catcher, he quickly looks at the batter, who either holds up one hand to signify "Stop!" or waves frantically as if to say, "Go! Go! Go!" When the runner races toward home plate, the on-deck hitter moves into his line of vision and lets him know whether or not to slide.

THE VALUE OF SPEED

A fast base runner is not necessarily a good base runner; he can make a poor decision that costs his team several runs, while a slowpoke with good baseball instincts can be a hero. But a dumb fast guy is still fast, and when he steps into the batter's box, everything changes:

- The pitcher throws more strikes to avoid walking him.

- The third baseman plays closer to home plate to guard against a bunt, and the middle infielders move in to prevent the batter from *beating out* a routine grounder. This reduces their *range* and makes it easier for the grounder to sneak past them.

- The fielders become more likely to make an error because they rush to make the play.

When a fast runner reaches base, he continues to disturb the defense:

- The pitcher, distracted by keeping an eye on him, becomes more likely to miss the catcher's target.

- The first baseman *holds the runner on,* and the middle infielders play closer to second base so they can beat him there if he tries to steal. This creates holes in the infield.

- Because faster pitches give the catcher a better chance to throw out the runner on a stolen base attempt, the hitter can *sit on a fastball*.

- When the runner reaches scoring position, the outfielders might play shallower to increase their chances of throwing him out at the plate. This helps the batter by making a *gapper* more likely to land for extra bases.

BASE-STEALING

Think about the ways in which a runner can advance from one base to the next: hit, walk, hit by pitch, error, *wild pitch,* passed ball, sacrifice bunt, sacrifice fly, groundout, *fielder's choice,* balk, *catcher's interference,* and *defensive indifference.* You know what they all have in common? The runner needs someone else to do something; either the hitter has to hit the ball or a fielder has to be involved. But there is one way for the runner to advance on his own: a stolen base. How does he do it? He takes his lead, waits until the pitcher pitches, sprints toward the next base, and slides ahead of the catcher's throw. It's exciting. It's risky. It takes just three seconds and ends with a *bang-bang play,* but both teams put a lot of thought into it.

Most people blame the catcher when a runner steals, but the pitcher is really the one who controls the running game: if he allows the runner to get a good jump, the catcher won't be able to throw him out. Normally, the pitcher pitches from the *windup* to establish his rhythm, shift his weight, and throw as hard as possible. But the windup takes three or four seconds— easily enough time for the runner to coast into the next base— so the pitcher shortens his delivery and throws from the stretch, possibly using a *slide step* instead of a time-consuming leg kick. This reduces his velocity, but limits the runner's jump. (Some relievers pitch from the stretch with the bases empty because they're used to entering the game with men on base and prefer to keep their mechanics consistent.)

As the runner inches off the bag, he keeps his feet spread and his weight balanced. He knows that the pitcher might throw over any time, so he stays in a slight crouch, avoids crossing his legs, and remains close enough to dart back with just one step and a dive. He also tries to time his jump by studying the pitcher and looking for a pattern in the length of time that he holds his set position. (On a *delayed steal*, the runner doesn't need to outsmart the pitcher. Instead, he tries to catch the middle infielders out of position by running just after the pitch.)

The pitcher can mess up the runner's timing by stepping off the rubber or varying the length of his pre-pitch pause. But if he takes too long, he might mess up his own timing if the hitter gets distracted and requests a time-out from the umpire. The pitcher can also *hold the runner* with a simple pick-off move. That's why he'll casually step off the rubber and lob a wimpy throw to the first baseman. He's not trying to fool anyone. He just wants to remind the runner that he's thinking about him in order to discourage him from leaning toward second. He also wants to save his best pick-off move for when it really matters. (The best pitchers often have the worst moves because they're not used to dealing with base runners.)

The first-base coach has several important duties:

- After a hitter reaches base, the coach congratulates him by patting him on the butt. Then the coach holds his unneeded shin and elbow guards.

- Using a stopwatch, the coach measures the time between the start of the pitcher's delivery and the moment that the ball reaches the catcher (about one and a half seconds). Then he adds it to the catcher's *glove-to-glove*—the time (about two seconds) it takes the catcher to catch a pitch and throw it to second base. Finally, the coach gives the combined time to the runner. The runner then knows whether he can make it because he will have already timed his own sprint down the baseline.

- The coach studies the pitcher's pick-off moves and helps the runner by yelling, "Back!" when he sees one coming.

The runner needs extra help when taking his lead against a left-handed pitcher because a lefty's leg kick can look the same before a pitch as it does before a pick-off throw. If the runner freezes (which is the natural reaction), he loses his chance to steal second and risks getting nabbed at first. Therefore, he must guess when the pitcher will throw home and then take off on first movement. This gives the runner a great jump, but leaves him vulnerable. (When you see the replay of a stolen base attempt, count how many steps the runner got before the pitcher released the ball. A good standard distance is three steps.)

The rule book, of course, says nothing about eye contact. Imagine how surprised you'd be if the pitcher kicked his leg, looked toward the catcher, and suddenly fired the ball in your direction. On the other hand, would you feel comfortable enough to start running if the pitcher kicked his leg while looking right at you? Many major leaguers don't, and they head back to first as the ball flies home.

What about stealing third? Is it easier or harder than stealing second? It depends on who you ask. The catcher's throw is 37 feet shorter, but the runner might feel more confident because he can get a *walking lead* and a bigger jump off second. That's because the middle infielders can't abandon their positions to hold the runner on, though the shortstop can creep in and smack his glove to make a noise that'll scare the runner and force him to shorten his lead.

The most effective pick-off move at second—the *daylight play*—is also the most difficult to execute. The shortstop dashes toward the base, forcing the runner to bolt there too. The pitcher looks for "daylight" between the two of them, and he'll see it if the shortstop passes the runner. Then, before the shortstop even reaches the bag, the pitcher whirls and throws. (The pitcher can't wait for the shortstop to get there because the runner is half a step behind him. Or less.) Sometimes the ball ends up in center field—after all, it's not so easy to catch either. And while thinking about all of this, the pitcher must remember to step off the rubber if he doesn't see daylight, because otherwise the play won't work and he needs to give his fielder time to get back into position.

If the hitter intentionally interferes with the catcher when he's trying to throw out a base stealer, the runner automatically gets called out. But the hitter's mere presence can create a legal obstacle. Every catcher throws right-handed[1] and therefore has a slightly tougher throw to second with a lefty at bat because the batter blocks his throwing lane. The same is true for a throw to third with a righty at bat. As a result, managers try to arrange their lineups with fast players in front of lefties (since second base is stolen more often), and runners consider who's batting before taking off.

Ty Cobb, fourth all time with 892 stolen bases, began his

---

[1]There have been 30 left-handed catchers in major league history, starting with Bill Harbridge, who caught 24 games for the Hartford Dark Blues in 1876. Jack Clements, whose career ended in 1900, holds the record with 1,073 games. Benny DiStefano became the last when he appeared behind the plate in three games for the 1989 Pirates.

career in 1905 and stole home a record 54 times. Rickey Henderson, first all time with 1,406 steals, started playing in 1979 and swiped home just four times. Although stealing home is a lost art, players still do it in two ways. The first combines a double steal and delayed steal: with runners on the corners, the trail runner takes off, and when the catcher throws to second, the *lead runner* races home ahead of the middle infielder's return throw. It sounds easy, but the catcher can prevent it. Sometimes, with runners on the corners, he steps in front of the plate and gives signs to let his infielders know which of these options he'll use:

- Faking a throw to second to lure the lead runner off third

- Throwing toward second, where a middle infielder cuts off the ball and quickly fires it home

- Throwing directly to second or third

- Holding the ball

The other way to steal home is a *straight steal*. The only way it can happen is if the pitcher uses a full windup because he foolishly assumes that the runner isn't going anywhere.

HIT-AND-RUN

The hit-and-run is a common—but daring—baserunning play designed to increase the batter's chance of getting a hit while giving a head start to the runner on first so he can make it to third on a single, score on a double, or avoid a double play. Here's how it works. The runner takes off as if he's stealing, and when the shortstop or second baseman leaves his position to cover second for the catcher's throw, the batter tries to smack a ground ball through the vacated hole in the infield. That's it. (Maybe it should be called the "run-and-hit.")

When it works, the hit-and-run looks simple, but things can easily go wrong. If the batter misses the sign from the third-base coach and stands there like a dummy, the runner is dead. Why? Because he's not actually trying to steal the base, so he takes a slightly shorter lead to avoid getting picked off and waits a fraction of a second longer before running. At the very least, the batter must protect him by swinging, even if the pitch bounces in the dirt or sails two feet over his head. This prevents the catcher from pouncing too soon.

After sprinting a few steps, the runner peeks toward home plate to *pick up the ball*. If he doesn't know where the batter has hit it, he might end up running on a fly ball when he should be scurrying back to his base. But if the batter has hit a bullet right at somebody, it doesn't matter if the runner sees it or not: it'll be an automatic double play if he's already halfway to second.

Because hitters often pull the ball, the second baseman usually covers second with a righty at bat. This is no secret. It's a common defensive strategy. Therefore, on a hit-and-run, a righty tries to poke the ball between first and second. This is a common offensive strategy, so the pitcher and catcher try to jam the hitter if they think the play is on. (Remember, it's tough to hit an inside pitch to the opposite field.) How would they know? The best time to attempt it is in a close game with a reasonably fast runner on first and a contact hitter at the plate. In this situation, the best count is 2-1 because the hitter can expect a pitch within the strike zone, or at least close to it. The pitcher doesn't want to fall further behind, so he won't try to foil the play with a pitchout because the count would slip to 3-1. So why not wait and try the hit-and-run on 3-1? That's when the pitcher is likely to throw a *BP fastball;* the hitter shouldn't waste it by protecting the runner with a puny grounder.

The middle infielders can trick the hitter by reversing their coverage. When there's a runner on first, they communicate before every pitch by using facial expressions to establish who'll take the throw: a closed mouth (in the "mmm" position) means, "I'm covering," and an open mouth means, "You got it." Of course, they shield their faces with their gloves so the other team can't see them.

SQUEEZE

The squeeze play (or *safety squeeze*) is a sacrifice bunt with a runner on third. When the runner takes off before the pitch, the play is called a *suicide squeeze* because it's do-or-die:

- If the batter misses the sign or fails to make contact, the runner will get caught between bases. (To prevent mis-communication, the third-base coach gives a visual sign to the batter and verbal instructions to the runner. The batter then gives a subtle return sign to show that he knows the plan.)

- If the runner reveals the play by taking off too soon, the pitcher might intentionally hit the batter, creating a *dead ball,* which forces the runner back to third.

- If the batter pops up, it's an easy double play.

Risky, yes. But there are two advantages. First, the runner is virtually guaranteed to score if the batter lays down even a mediocre bunt. Second, the only way for the defense to thwart the play is to predict it and pitch out.

Teams rarely squeeze with no outs because they still have a chance for a big inning. With two outs, of course, the play wouldn't work because the inning would end with the bunter being thrown out at first base.

HUSTLE

We see it all the time: the batter hits a *come-backer* or a routine pop-up, flips his bat, and jogs halfheartedly toward first because he assumes the fielder will make the play. Or he mashes a deep fly and begins his home run trot because he's sure that the ball's not coming back. Well, sometimes it does come back. Sometimes the other team *boots* it. Sometimes Mr. Big Shot gets thrown out at first by half a step or has to stop at second when he could have hustled to third.

Inconceivably, some players lack the motivation and desire to sprint *90 feet* four times a day. These guys have multimillion-dollar contracts. They have 24 teammates. They have thousands of adoring fans in the stands who don't pay to watch Grandpa take his evening stroll.

But before you dis all joggers, consider that a base runner has to wait on a ball hit in the air with less than two outs, so the batter might not gain anything by racing down the line. Also, some guys play through minor injuries, which don't stop them from hitting and catching and throwing as they normally would but do prevent them from running full speed. Toward the end of his impressive career, Mariners designated hitter Edgar Martinez probably looked lazy to fans who didn't know that he had such fragile *hamstrings* that he had doctor's orders not to run hard.

CHAPTER 5
FIELDING

If a woman has to choose between catching a fly ball and saving an infant's life, she will choose to save the infant's life without even considering if there are men on base.

—Dave Barry, humorist

DEFENSIVE ALIGNMENT

No one can predict where the ball is heading, but a major league fielder's experience often gives him a hunch. He assumes that the number-nine hitter won't whack a 400-foot fly ball. He knows that the cleanup batter won't bunt. He realizes when the other team needs to manufacture a run with a *sac fly* or a grounder to the right side. He remembers who hits where and positions himself accordingly.

But what if a rookie steps to the plate, and none of the fielders know anything about him? What if a tense situation requires an unusual defensive alignment? That's when a coach climbs to the top step of the dugout and, combining his own experience with the information from his charts and scouting reports, moves his fielders by gesturing like a traffic cop. He might send an outfielder back or to the side, bring the infield in, or just move the corners in. He might tell his first baseman to play behind the runner instead of holding him on. Or he might use one of these extreme plays:

THE TED WILLIAMS SHIFT Popularized in the 1940s by Indians shortstop-manager Lou Boudreau, who used it against Williams, the shift moves fielders to the right side of the infield to guard against the extreme pull-hitting tendencies of left-handed sluggers. The third baseman stands where the shortstop normally plays, the shortstop moves to the right side of second, the second baseman plays shallow right field, and the first baseman *hugs the line*. Sometimes the outfielders move too.

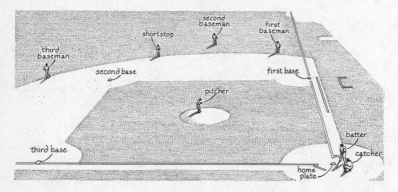

In recent years, teams have used the shift—now commonly referred to as the *overshift*—against sluggers like Barry Bonds, Carlos Delgado, Rafael Palmeiro, David Ortiz, Jason Giambi, Jim Thome, and Ken Griffey Jr. Like Williams, current players rarely change their approach; they see the shift as an insult or a challenge to hit the ball even harder. On very rare occasions, you might see one of these guys put his ego aside and bunt down the unguarded third-base line.

THE WHEEL PLAY This play sets the entire infield in motion to prevent a runner from advancing from second to third base on a sacrifice bunt. As the pitch is thrown, the first and third basemen charge toward the plate, and the middle infielders sprint to first and third. The goal is to reach the bunted ball quickly while covering the only two spots—first and third—where there could be a play. Since the wheel play opens the entire infield, the defense better be sure that a bunt is on the way.

THE NO-DOUBLES DEFENSE This helps protect a small late-inning lead by making it tougher for the batter to stroke an extra-base hit. The first and third basemen hug the lines, and the outfielders play deep to prevent anything (except a home run) from being hit over their heads. Unfortunately, this alignment often becomes a "more-singles defense" as routine grounders and shallow fly balls find holes.

SHALLOW OUTFIELD When the winning run is at third with less than two outs in the bottom of the ninth, the outfielders play so shallow that they look like Little Leaguers on a grown-up field. This makes it easy for a routine fly ball to sail over their heads and win the game—but a routine fly ball, if caught, would still be a game-winning sac fly. One of the outfielders might move all the way in to help the drawn-in infield prevent a grounder from sneaking through.

RIGHTIES AND LEFTIES

Remember why a manager prefers to have a lefty at bat when his runner tries to steal a base? It's because a lefty stands in the catcher's throwing lane and partially blocks his throw. This is why you probably won't ever see a left-handed catcher. He'd be blocked by righties—and there are far more of those than lefties. You'll also never see a lefty playing second base, third base, or shortstop, because he'd be facing the wrong way—away from first base—after fielding a grounder.

Pitchers and outfielders can be right- or left-handed, as can a first baseman. In fact, a lefty first baseman has three advantages:

- When he catches a pick-off throw and tries to tag the runner, he has a shorter distance to move his glove than a righty, who must reach across his body.

- More balls are hit to his right, his glove side, so he doesn't have to make as many backhanded plays.

- He's already facing second and third base after fielding the ball, so he can throw to them quicker than a righty, who first has to do some fancy footwork.

HOW MANY OUTS?

A fielder who doesn't know how many outs there are could hurt his team. If he thinks there's only one out, he might needlessly attempt to nail the lead runner instead of making the easy play at first.[1]

Though tempted to look at the scoreboard to stay informed, he and his teammates help each other by holding up one or

---

[1] That's nothing compared to the blunder by Expos right fielder Larry Walker at Dodger Stadium in 1994. He caught a fly ball near the foul line and, thinking the inning was over, handed it to a child in the first row. But it was only the second out, and the runner on first advanced two bases on his error. Two Mets left fielders made the same mistake at Shea Stadium—Benny Agbayani in 2000 and Cliff Floyd in 2004— and several other players have done it since. Duh.

two fingers (or occasionally a fist, if they're not too embar-
rassed to remind themselves that they haven't yet recorded an
out) after each play. That's because the scoreboard operator
can make an error too.

BACK THAT BASE UP

Bad throws are inevitable, even in the Major Leagues, even on
routine plays. Therefore, when a fielder is not directly involved
in a play, he often leaves his position to back up his teammates
so he'll be able to pounce on the ball if it gets loose and prevent the runner from advancing.

This is one of those things that's easier to see in person than
on TV, so the next time you're at a game, don't keep your eye on
the ball. Instead, watch the catcher sprint down the first-base
line on a routine grounder with the bases empty. Watch the left
fielder move toward the foul line when a runner tries to steal
third. Watch the pitcher rush toward the *backstop* before a play
at the plate. It's even worth checking out the third baseman
after a pick-off attempt at first. Occasionally, he'll jog in a few
steps to back up the first baseman's easy toss to the pitcher.

IT *IS* POLITE TO POINT

Fans wear white T-shirts. The sky has white clouds. The batter
hits a white ball, and the fielders often struggle to see it, especially when it sails in front of the sun or the stadium lights.

The pitcher and infielders point at a pop-up to help each
other locate the ball. If a fielder still can't see it, he shrugs
and sticks out his arms. That's body language for "*Help!!!*" and
his closest teammate races over to try to make the play.

"I GOT IT! I GOT IT! YOU TAKE IT!"

The batter bloops the ball toward the *Bermuda Triangle*. The outfielders run in. The infielders run out. Everybody's looking up. The center fielder yells, "I got it!" but his words get drowned out by 55,437 shrieking fans and a jet flying overhead. Doesn't matter. The Dominican second baseman and Japanese shortstop don't speak much English anyway. Best-case scenario: no one gets hurt.

Luckily, on routine fly balls and towering pop-ups, there are guidelines that determine which fielder has the right of way:

- Any outfielder has priority over any infielder. (It's easier to make a catch while running forward than backward.)

- The center fielder has priority over the other outfielders.

- The shortstop has priority over the other infielders.

- The first and third basemen have priority over the catcher.

- The pitcher has no priority. He should get out of the way and leave the fielding to the real athletes.

THE INFIELD FLY RULE

Picture this: The bases are loaded with no outs, and the batter hits one *up the elevator shaft*. All three runners trot back to their bases and wait for the catcher to make the play—except that he lets the ball hit the ground in fair territory, creating an unexpected force at every base. The runners take off, but it's too late, as the catcher has already stepped on the plate for the first out of what will be a *triple play*.

Not fair.

That's why the *infield fly rule* was invented. It prevents the defense from taking advantage of a routine infield pop-up with less than two outs and runners on first and second or with the bases loaded.

When the umpire declares, "Infield fly!" the batter is automatically out (the defense doesn't even have to catch the ball), and the runners can advance at their own risk. This means they can stay on their bases if the ball is dropped or tag up if it's caught.[2]

DEFENSIVE INDIFFERENCE

You're the manager. It's the ninth inning, and you have a three-run lead. The other team is batting with one out. The runner on first wants to reach scoring position to eliminate the force and avoid a double play. Since one run won't cost you the game, you *call time,* walk to the mound, and tell your pitcher to focus on the hitter. Then you instruct your first baseman to play behind the runner, who predictably takes off on the next pitch. The catcher holds the ball, and the runner cruises into second without a slide. He's happy. You don't care. The official scorer notes that he advanced on defensive indifference and does not credit him with a stolen base.

[2]The infield fly rule is important, even though it'll affect your team only once or twice a week. Most fans don't know how it works and could use a gentle explanation. Many others use it as the benchmark of baseball aptitude and will quiz you on it, boosting their own egos in the process. Don't let them get away with it. Show them how little they know. Ask them what year the rule was instituted (1895). Ask them whether the rule can take effect on a popped-up bunt (nope). Ask them what happens if the ump declares, "Infield fly!" and the ball lands in foul territory (the hitter stays at bat). With infield fly brats as the one exception, you should use your baseball knowledge for good and not evil.

APPEAL

If the defense thinks that a runner left his base too early on a sacrifice fly or missed a base entirely, a fielder waits for the play to end and then either tags him or touches the base to get the ump to call him out. This is called an *appeal*. It rarely works.

But it worked in 1962 at the Polo Grounds when "Marvelous" Marv Throneberry, the bumbling but beloved first baseman for the pitiful Mets, hit an apparent triple but was called out for missing second base. When his manager, Casey Stengel,[3] ran onto the field, first-base coach Cookie Lavagetto stopped him and said, "Don't bother arguing. He missed first base too."

PLAYING OUTFIELD

Outfield walls in early ballparks weren't padded like they are now. Today the outfielders even have a dirt lane in front called a *warning track*. So when a fielder races after a deep fly with his eye on the ball, the ground crunches under his spikes, warning him to slow down so he doesn't break his head.

Walls aside, you might think it's easy for a major league outfielder to catch a fly ball—and it usually is. He wears a bigger glove than the infielders, stands a safer distance from home plate, and doesn't have to deal with bad hops.

Right?

Wrong.

[3]Stengel, inducted into the Hall of Fame four years later, is the only manager to win five consecutive World Series. He accomplished the feat with the Yankees from 1949 to 1953. Of his '62 Mets, who finished 40-120 and remain the worst team since 1900, Stengel said, "They have shown me ways to lose I never knew existed."

Occasionally, fly balls travel in crazy, unexpected ways: when a pitch meets the bat just right, the ball can shoot off without spin and speed like a 117-mph knuckleball. An outfielder must also field grounders—which can take bad hops even on seemingly perfect grass—and play the ball as it deflects unpredictably off various objects and surfaces like wood, padding, brick, ivy, scoreboards, tarpaulins, ball boys' stools, bullpen mounds, benches, railings, fences, and ladders.[4] He also has to deal with wind and sun and avoid crashing into his teammates while staying focused on the ball even when it momentarily disappears while passing in front of stadium lights or a white dome overhead—often while running full speed.

But which way should he run? Forget about keeping his eye on the ball. Just figuring out where it's heading is tough enough. Sometimes on a clear day he looks up and loses his depth perception; without clouds, there's nothing behind the ball for him to use as a reference point in order to judge its trajectory. In addition, he stands so far from home plate that he doesn't get a close-up view of the bat hitting the ball, so he has to use the batter's swing to figure out how hard it's been hit. Of course, when a *heavy hitter* takes a mighty *hack* but merely bloops one off the end of the bat, it causes all kinds of confusion. And if the outfielder pauses for a split second in order to figure out any of this, he'll be criticized for getting a bad jump.

Even after he figures out where the ball is heading, he needs to make some quick decisions. If it's hit directly over his head, should he turn left or right as he races back? (If he turns one way and then the other, it means he's misjudged it.)

---

[4]Actually, there's only one ladder that's *in play* in all of Major League Baseball. It's mounted to the *Green Monster* at Fenway Park. (You'll learn more about Fenway and the Monster in the next chapter.)

If it's hit in front of him, should he play it safe and field it on a bounce? Should he try to make a *shoestring catch?* Should he dive? If so, feet-first or head-first? If he dives and misses the ball, can his team afford to let the runner take an extra base or two? It all depends on the situation. Inning? Score? Outs? On-deck hitter? Base runners?

Ahh, base runners. When there's more than one, the outfielder must not act like a tough guy by launching the ball all the way to his target on a fly. Instead, he needs to throw it low enough for the *cutoff man*—the infielder who relays the throw—to snag it, preferably on his glove side so he can make the catch and quick release in one motion. If the outfielder misses the cutoff man, the runners will see that the throw is too high to be cut off, and one of them—usually the trail runner—will keep moving, knowing he won't be thrown out as the ball sails above the infield.

But where should the outfielder throw it? Go for the lead runner? Hold the trail runner? Again, it depends on the situation, and he needs to plan it before the pitcher *toes the rubber.* Not only must he decide where to throw, but he must also catch the ball with his momentum moving toward his target. For example, when a runner prepares to tag up on a routine fly, the outfielder stays several steps behind the spot where the ball will land so he can wait until the last second, charge, and use a *crow hop* to gain extra velocity on his throw. If he uses both hands and catches the ball directly above his throwing arm, he'll save time by being closer to throwing position.

Sometimes the outfielder needs to know when *not* to catch the ball. Let's say the game is tied with one out in the bottom of the ninth and there's a runner on third. If the batter lifts a fly ball down the line, the outfielder must have the presence of mind to let it drop if it's in foul territory so that the runner can't tag up and score the winning run.

PLAYING INFIELD

Infielders hate bad hops. So do groundskeepers. Bad hops make everyone look bad, but they're inevitable. It doesn't matter how many times the dirt is raked or how carefully the grass is mowed and watered. Just about anything—a runner's footprint, the *lip* where the grass meets the dirt, a pea-sized pebble, or a random unlucky piece of earth—can cause the ball to bounce unpredictably. Even on *AstroTurf,* the ball can hit a seam and bounce funny—maybe not funny enough to knock out an infielder's front teeth, or worse, to scoot through his legs; maybe not funny enough for you or even the official scorer to notice; but funny enough to make the ball come up an extra two inches and kick off the heel of his glove. So don't scream at your TV or grumble that the player belongs in the minors. At least wait to see if he can redeem himself at the plate next inning.

Whether or not the ball takes a bad hop, the fielder can make it easier to catch if he predicts how far in front of him it'll hit the ground and then moves accordingly. Why move at all? Because he should never be caught flat-footed; he should play the ball instead of letting the ball play him.

Here are the three main types of bounces, rated in terms of difficulty on a scale of one (routine) to ten (impossible):

- *Room service hop*—Well, come on, what's easier than room service? This is the kind of ground ball that lands well in front of the fielder and bounces waist- or chest-high. He has plenty of time to react if the ball takes a bad hop. Difficulty rating: 1.1

- *Short hop*—It might look fancy when the fielder swipes his glove and scoops the ball in one motion, but when the ball lands at (or near) his feet, he can practically smother it before it has a chance to bounce off in some crazy direction. Difficulty rating: 2.3

- *In-between hop*—This is the dreaded ball that lands too close for the fielder to react, but too far for him to scoop up. All he can do is stick out his glove where he thinks it'll bounce and pray to the ground ball gods. Difficulty rating: 7.4[5]

Of course, the speed of the hitter is even more important. What if the fielder waits for a nice big bounce but doesn't have enough time to nail the guy at first? He still has to throw the ball to record an out—and juggle other critical factors in his head at the same time. When there's an open base and he has a spare moment after snaring a hard grounder, he quickly peeks at the runner before throwing to first to prevent him from advancing. In addition, he gives his throw a straight, crisp path by looking at the ball—or feeling it in his glove—to get a four-seam grip. (Remember how to hold a four-seam fastball?)

Fielding grounders and firing them across the *diamond* are just the beginning of the infielder's job. The following sections break down the other duties and challenges position by position.

THE PITCHER

"I was never nervous when I had the ball," said Hall-of-Fame pitcher Lefty Gomez, "but when I let go I was scared to death."

He might not have been joking.

---

[5]Difficulty rating for kids who play on public fields that have no groundskeepers: 9.9

Don't overlook the pitcher's defensive ability just because he gets paid to throw the ball. As soon as he lets it fly, he becomes a fielder at a frighteningly short distance from the batter—less than 55 feet by the time he follows through. He needs to finish his delivery in a ready position, not only to play good defense but to protect himself from line drives, which travel much faster than the fastest fastballs. Ready or not, many pitchers get hit. One of the scariest moments came in 1957 when Indians left-hander Herb Score was drilled on the right eye by a wicked line drive off the bat of Yankees infielder Gil McDougald. Score was 23 years old, and his promising career was virtually ruined.

HERB SCORE'S CAREER STATS

TWO+ YEARS BEFORE LINE DRIVE	FIVE YEARS AFTER LINE DRIVE
38 wins, 20 losses	17 wins, 26 losses
.655 winning percentage	.395 winning percentage
547 strikeouts	290 strikeouts
2.63 ERA	4.43 ERA

Even if the ball isn't hit quite as hard as it was in this case, and even if the pitcher thinks he might be able to glove it, he's sometimes better off fighting his reflexes and letting it go. A chopper up the middle is often a routine play for the shortstop, but it becomes an infield hit when the pitcher helplessly stabs at the ball and deflects it into no-man's-land.

Even before the pitch—even before holding the base runners close and getting the sign from the catcher—the pitcher needs to look at his teammates to make sure they're ready. Is the right fielder tying his shoes? Is the third baseman smoothing out clumps of dirt? Is the left fielder retrieving a loose beach ball? Is the center fielder trying to get a speck of dust out of his eye? Is the shortstop still dancing behind second base for a pick-off throw? If so, the batter has a huge advantage.

In a double-play situation, the pitcher communicates with his middle infielders to find out who will cover second base on a come-backer. Pay close attention right after the runner reaches first base, and you might see the pitcher turn toward second and point at one of his guys. Usually, the shortstop takes the throw, but the pitcher makes sure so he won't fire the ball to the wrong side of the base. If there's a runner on third, the pitcher must remember to cover the plate on a wild pitch or passed ball. And whether or not anyone's on base, he needs to cover first whenever a grounder to the right side pulls the first baseman out of position (a tough play because the pitcher has to catch the throw while looking for the base while running full speed while trying to avoid getting spiked by the runner).

Finally, the pitcher moves all these distractions to the back of his head so he can focus on making the right pitch with the right movement to the right location.

THE CATCHER

No catcher has ever caught all 162 games in a season—and probably no one ever will. Randy Hundley came the closest with 160 for the 1968 Cubs, but a number that high would be unheard of today. Managers now prefer to rest their catchers one or two days a week in order to keep them fresh later in the season—not a bad idea when you're dealing with the guy who knows the tendencies of every hitter in the league, chooses the pitches, controls the running game, instructs his teammates where to throw the ball because he can see the entire field, sprints down the first-base line to back up the first baseman, serves as a part-time psychologist for the pitching staff, eases tension with home-plate umpires, pounces on bunts, races after wild pitches, and chases pop-ups.

Pop-ups. Not easy. When the batter hits one behind the plate, the ball has tremendous backspin and drifts back toward fair territory. First, the catcher yanks off his mask to give himself a better view. Then he turns his back to the field to prepare for the ball's reverse descent. Finally, after *camping under it,* he flings his mask far away so he won't trip over it if he moves a few feet to make the catch. Plus he has to avoid tripping over the weighted bats in the on-deck circle, slamming into the backstop, or crashing down the dugout steps, especially at the other team's dugout where the players won't exactly jump off the bench to pad his landing.

Of all players, the catcher's body takes the most serious beating. How serious? Try this at home: Crouch. (That's right. Get up. You can take the book with you. Okay, are you crouching now? C'mon, no cheating. Go all the way down until your butt is practically touching your heels. Good.) Now hold it there. Don't move yet. Okay, stand up. Crouch again. Wait. Keep waiting. Count slowly to five. Stand up. Crouch. Wait. Just a few more seconds. And a few more. Stand up. Crouch. Wait. Wait some more. Stand up. Pretty tiring, right? Imagine how tired the catcher feels. He has to do it about 150 times a day, five or six days a week, six months a year. Whoops, almost forgot Spring Training. That's another month and a half. Oh yeah, how about the playoffs? Add a few more weeks. And hey, why not throw in some winter ball in Central America? All this time he gets hit by *foul tips,* whacked with bats, and pummeled by aggressive base runners.

The rule book allows the catcher to block the plate, but he better hold the ball tight because the runner is allowed to smash him. The most famous collision in baseball history took place in the bottom of the 12th inning of the 1970 All-Star

Game when Reds outfielder Pete Rose rammed Indians catcher Ray Fosse, knocked the ball out of his glove, and scored the winning run. Fosse sustained a fractured shoulder, and Rose was criticized for his aggressive play in what many people felt was a meaningless exhibition game.

Collisions are scary. So is crouching right behind the hitter, but the catcher must stay close to home plate so he can catch breaking balls before—or right after—they bounce. At the same time, he must stay far enough back so the batter's swing won't hit him. If it does, he gets charged with an error for catcher's interference, and the batter goes to first base (without being charged for an at-bat so his average doesn't drop).

When you consider all the ways that a catcher can get hurt, it's no wonder that people call his equipment the *tools of ignorance*. Yeah, these tools help keep him alive, but dealing with them is a burden. Throughout the game, he has to remove them before his at-bats and replace them before returning to the field. The chest protector and shin guards— each piece with several straps, hooks, and clasps—take the most time, so he wears them in the dugout when he's pretty sure he won't bat in a particular inning. But if he's due up fourth or fifth and doesn't know whether he'll bat, he removes the chest protector and leaves the shin guards on so that he's semiprepared either way. (Sometimes you'll see him wear the guards in the on-deck circle with two outs.) The biggest hassle comes after he makes the third out or gets left on base at the end of an inning. That's when he has to hurry back to the dugout and get ready all over again while a backup catcher or coach warms up the pitcher.

Despite all this equipment, there's nothing that protects his throwing hand, so he keeps it behind his back whenever possible. Unfortunately, he can't do this with runners on base because he'd lose time before throwing. If he doesn't need to throw, and if the pitch is *on the black,* he *frames* it by moving his glove slightly toward the strike zone. Then he holds still so the ump will get a good view and hopefully call it a strike. When he throws back to the pitcher, he needs to be accurate; if the pitcher has to jump, reach, lean, or bend unexpectedly, he could lose his focus or even pull a muscle. But the pitcher is less likely to return the favor of throwing accurately. When he chucks a 55-*footer,* the catcher doesn't actually try to catch the ball. Instead, he tries to block it by dropping to his knees, closing the space between his legs with his glove and arms, and absorbing the impact with his chest protector. It's difficult. It hurts. But if he can do it, especially with a runner on third, the pitcher will love him forever.

THE FIRST BASEMAN

Yes, it's true. A power-hitting meathead with no defensive skills often ends up playing first base. He'll catch a few pop-ups and grounders. He'll hold the runners close. He'll take throws from other infielders. And he'll usually succeed if he's simply trying not to embarrass himself. But stick a great fielder there, and he'll bring beauty and grace to the many challenges of this overlooked position.

The first challenge is standing in the right spot. If the first baseman plays too close to the bag, he widens the hole for the hitter. If he plays too far away, he can't get back in time to set himself and use proper footwork before catching his teammates' throws. By keeping one foot on the bag and reaching out as the ball approaches, he can shave almost ten feet—and possibly a tenth of a second—off the throw.

Since a right-handed pitcher can't see first base from his set position, the first baseman lets him know when he's going to play behind the runner so there won't be an accidental pick-off throw with no one covering. When the first baseman does hold the runner, he has to read the pitcher's pick-off move so he doesn't move off the bag too soon, and he must stay alert for a *snap throw* from the catcher.

Everyone makes bad throws, even *Gold Glovers*. The first baseman needs to catch them. When the ball falls short, he scoops it. When a throw is too high, he jumps, makes the catch, and lands on the base in one fluid motion. When a throw misses wide, he lunges for it and tags the runner. When a throw is so wild that there's little chance of completing the play, he ignores the runner, comes off the bag, and tries to block the ball.

The first baseman also has to field ground balls (he sees more bad hops than anyone because of all the foot traffic near his position) and deal with his own throws. When he's pulled out of position by a grounder and the pitcher sprints over, the first baseman leads him to the bag with a chest-high toss. (In case you've never tried it, it's not easy to hit a moving target.) When there's a play at second, the first baseman steps forward—to the inside of the baseline—before throwing. This gives him a clear target so he won't hit the runner. Sometimes he must become the clear target; when a dropped third strike scoots behind the plate, he stands in foul territory—with one foot on the bag—so the catcher's throw doesn't have to cross the baseline (see the illustration on page 93).

When the opposing pitcher comes to bat with a runner on first and less than two outs, everyone in the ballpark (even the hot dog vendors) knows he's going to bunt. Sometimes the first baseman charges just before the pitch is thrown, putting himself dangerously close to the plate but in a great position

to snag the bunt and throw out the lead runner. If the batter pops up and doesn't run hard because he assumes his pathetic bloop will be caught, the first baseman can let it drop and *turn two* by creating a force play at both bases. (Remember, the infield fly rule doesn't apply to bunts.)

The first baseman has several other responsibilities. On an extra-base hit, he watches the runner to make sure he touches first base. On any hit to right or center field that results in a play at the plate, he races toward the mound, lines himself up between the outfielder and catcher, and serves as the cutoff man. To snare a pop-up in foul territory, he sometimes has to dodge various obstacles such as tarpaulins, photographers' boxes, television cameras, dugout steps, railings, and ball-hungry fans.

Finally, you can't talk about first base without mentioning Bill Buckner. Buckner had a great career (with more hits than Ted Williams, more stolen bases than Roberto Clemente, and more sacrifice flies than Willie Mays), but everybody remembers him for one thing: playing first base for the Red Sox in the 1986 World Series, he made the most costly error of all time. It was the 10th inning of Game 6 when he let Mookie Wilson's weak grounder trickle under his glove and through his legs, allowing the winning run to score.[6] Two days later, the Mets won Game 7, and the *Curse of the Bambino* had struck again.

THE SECOND BASEMAN

Some people will tell you that second base is a wimpy position, that the guy who plays there is really just a shortstop with a lousy arm—and they might be right if they're talking about high school ball. But in the majors it's essential for a team to be strong up the middle. That's where most of the action takes place. The pitcher, catcher, center fielder, shortstop, and second baseman are the fielders who control the

---

[6]Six years later, actor Charlie Sheen bought this ball at an auction for $93,500. But that's not the most anyone's paid for a ball. Not even close. At an auction in 1999, comic book mogul Todd McFarlane spent $3.005 million for Mark McGwire's record-breaking 70th home run ball from the previous season.

game. As for the whole lousy arm thing, have you noticed how many *off-balance throws* the second baseman makes? Every time he *charges the ball* or ranges up the middle, his momentum carries him away from first base. Consider how hard it is and how much arm strength he needs to run in one direction and throw in another.

Harder still is turning a double play. First he races to second base in time for the throw. Then he catches it, touches the bag, and transfers the ball from his glove to his bare hand so fast that you can barely see him do it. (That's why middle infielders wear the smallest gloves on the team. If they wore big ones like the outfielders, they'd need more time to get a good grip on the ball after catching it.) Then he throws it to first base while trying to avoid the runner's takeout slide.

Watch the second baseman's footwork as he catches the ball and touches the bag. Normally, he steps toward first, but if the runner is right in his face, he needs to get fancy. His first option is to step forward or backward to the inside or outside of the baseline. This often tricks the runner into sliding to the wrong spot. His other option, which takes a split second longer, is to protect himself by staying on the far side of the bag and using it as a shield. The runner can't slide through it because it's firmly planted in the ground and sticks up several inches.

When the second baseman fields a *double-play ball,* he tries to give his shortstop a perfect chest-high throw in one of several ways. If he's in his normal position, he pivots and throws sidearm. If he's closer to first base, he spins 180 degrees counterclockwise and fires overhand. If he's near second, he makes a backhand flip or an underhand toss. If he's behind second (and needs to try something funky), he might fling the ball behind his back or directly from his glove.

If, however, he catches the ball in the right spot, he doesn't need to make any of these throws. He can simply tag the passing runner and throw directly to first.

Or can he?

In 1996 Brewers second baseman Fernando Vina grabbed a routine grounder and prepared to tag Indians outfielder Albert Belle, who'd been retired earlier in the game on an identical play. Belle (6-foot-2, 220 pounds), in an even worse mood than usual after having just been plunked intentionally, collided with Vina (5-foot-9, 170 pounds) and bashed him on the nose with his forearm. The benches emptied. Fists flew. The controversy erupted. The Brewers argued that Vina was viciously assaulted. The Indians claimed that Belle was simply trying to break up the double play. (He succeeded.) But the American League had the final word: Belle was suspended for three games and fined $25,000.

Here are a few other things the second baseman does. He covers first when a bunt pulls the first baseman out of position. He covers second on throws from the left and center fielders. He's the cutoff man when the right fielder throws to second. He shouts, "Going!" when a runner takes off from first so that the catcher knows the guy is stealing. (The catcher can't always see the runner, especially when there's a left-handed hitter who blocks his view of the right side of the field—another reason why a manager tries to arrange his lineup with a lefty after the speedster.) The second baseman covers second on stolen base attempts when there's a righty at bat. And when he—or any infielder—prepares to tag a runner with an incoming throw, he straddles the base. This blocks the edges and forces the runner to slide straight in. It also makes the second baseman more likely to get spiked. But he deserves it, right? He's a wimp with a lousy arm.

THE THIRD BASEMAN

Third base is called the *hot corner* because the action takes place just 90 feet from the batter. When a guy hits a hard grounder at the third baseman so fast that he can hardly react—let alone avoid an in-between hop—he tries to block it with his body. He knows that if he keeps the ball in front of him, he'll probably have time to snatch it and throw out the runner at first. Of course, he needs quick reflexes and a strong arm, not to mention a whole lot of courage and a protective cup.

He also needs to position himself just right. When a speedster steps into the box, the third baseman moves closer to the plate in case the guy bunts—but not too close or the batter will try to slap the ball past him (if not down his throat). To be safe, he plays *even with the bag,* where he's close enough to field most bunts, but far enough away to react to most line drives.

The most difficult play for the third baseman comes on a slow roller down the line. First he charges and grabs the ball with his bare hand. Then, with hardly any time to get a good grip, he throws off-balance (and sidearm) to first base while his momentum takes him toward the plate. This play is so tough that if the ball is hugging the line, he might just step aside and hope that it rolls foul. In a 1981 game at the Kingdome, Seattle's old ballpark with an AstroTurf field, Mariners third baseman Lenny Randle took this strategy one step further. Realizing he had no play on a *swinging bunt* by Royals center fielder Amos Otis, he got down on his hands and knees and blew the ball foul. The Royals protested, and the ump awarded Otis with a hit.

Normally, fielders don't cut in front of each other, but there's one play on which the third baseman is actually supposed to be a ball hog. When the batter sends a weak grounder toward the shortstop, the third baseman bolts to his left and tries to snag it because his momentum takes him more toward first base, and his throw will be shorter.

The third baseman has several other duties. He's the cutoff man on throws from left field to home plate. He covers third when a runner on second tries to steal. He deals with obstacles in foul territory when he chases pop-ups. And he's usually the guy who starts a triple play. It doesn't happen often, but when a really slow right-handed batter yanks a hard grounder down the line with no outs and runners on first and second, the third baseman grabs the ball, steps on the bag for the first out, fires to second for the second out, and watches his teammates do the rest.

THE SHORTSTOP

The shortstop is the leader of the infield and often the best athlete on the team. He needs to be. He gets more balls hit to him than anyone else, and most of them are grounders. As tough as grounders can be, they're even tougher for him because he has the smallest margin for error. Any other infielder can block or bobble a ball and still recover in time to throw out the runner at first. But the shortstop must field it cleanly because the combined distance of the hit and throw is longer for him than for anyone else. Think about it. The third baseman fields short grounders and makes long throws. The second baseman fields long grounders and makes short throws. But the shortstop fields long grounders *and* makes long throws.

His true athletic test comes on a deep grounder to the 5.5 *hole*. He needs to be quick enough to get there, agile enough to reverse his momentum after catching the ball, and strong enough to put some *mustard* on the long throw. Over the years, several players have used their own techniques to make this play. In the 1970s, Reds shortstop Dave Concepcion became the first to bounce the throw intentionally. This was practical and effective because he had the luxury (or curse, depending on how you look at it) of playing on the hard and smooth artificial surface of Riverfront Stadium. In the 1980s, Cardinals shortstop Ozzie Smith dove head-first at the ball and then immediately, almost impossibly, sprang back to his feet. In the 1990s, Mets shortstop Rey Ordonez slid feet-first as he caught the ball, then popped up and threw in one motion. These days, Yankees shortstop Derek Jeter stays on his feet for the catch, then jumps and twists his body and throws from midair.

Are these plays flashy? Without a doubt. Successful? Sometimes. Stupid? Occasionally. Despite the joy of appearing on the highlight reels, the shortstop needs to accept infield hits as part of the game. He must have the presence of mind, even during the most frenzied action, to realize when he has no chance and his best play is to catch the ball and *stick it in his back pocket.*

When the shortstop fields a double-play ball, he flips it to second base from a crouch or from his knees; there's no point in wasting a third of a second by standing up. When he covers second on a double play, he gets himself out of the baseline by skimming across the bag and barely clipping it—sometimes actually missing it—by dragging his right foot. This is called the *neighborhood play.* As long as he's in the neighborhood of second base, the ump will give him the call. But because the runner can slide slightly out of the baseline, the shortstop might still need to dodge him. If the runner has nearly reached the base, the shortstop has no choice but to throw the ball and try to jump over him. If the runner is several steps away, the shortstop stays low and throws sidearm, forcing him to slide early to avoid being hit in the you-know-what.

Let's say there's one out and a runner on first. Let's say the manager calls a hit-and-run, and the guy takes off for second. Let's say the guy runs with his head down, never looking back at the batter to pick up the ball. If the batter hits a pop-up or fly ball, the shortstop can trick the runner by pretending to field a grounder. The second baseman might get in on it too, scurrying toward the bag for the "throw." The runner, tricked into thinking that there's a force play, will keep running toward second (and possibly even slide to break up a nonexistent double play) instead of racing back to first to avoid getting *doubled off*.

The shortstop covers second on throws from right field. He's also the cutoff man on throws to second from left and center field, and with one exception, he cuts off all throws to third. When the right or center fielder makes a very long throw, the second baseman occasionally becomes the cutoff man, and the shortstop backs him up. He stays about 20 feet behind in case the outfielder's throw sails high or falls short. That way, the second baseman can let it go, knowing that the shortstop will catch it in a better throwing position.

THE GOLD GLOVE AWARD

In 1957 a company called Rawlings, the major maker of baseballs and gloves and other sporting goods equipment, began using fielding statistics to reward the best fielder at each position with a trophy adorned with a gold glove. The following year Rawlings gave the award to the two best fielders—one in each league—and the tradition stuck.

These days, managers and coaches select the winners by voting (they're not allowed to pick their own players), so stats no longer matter. As a result, fielders with high error totals can be chosen, but they often deserve it; better athletes tend to make more errors because their speed allows them to reach balls that slower players can only dream of catching.

Here are the top five Gold Glovers at each position and the number of times they've won:

Pitchers	Catchers	First Basemen	Second Basemen
Jim Kaat 16	Ivan Rodriguez 12	Keith Hernandez 11	Roberto Alomar 10
Greg Maddux 16	Johnny Bench 10	Don Mattingly 9	Ryne Sandberg 9
Bob Gibson 9	Bob Boone 7	George Scott 8	Bill Mazeroski 8
Bobby Shantz 8	Jim Sundberg 6	Vic Power 7	Frank White 8
Mark Langston 7	Bill Freehan 5	Bill White 7	Two tied with 5[7]

Third Basemen	Shortstops	Outfielders
Brooks Robinson 16	Ozzie Smith 13	Roberto Clemente 12
Mike Schmidt 10	Omar Vizquel 11	Willie Mays 12
Buddy Bell 6	Luis Aparicio 9	Ken Griffey Jr. 10
Scott Rolen 7	Mark Belanger 8	Al Kaline 10
Three tied with 6[8]	Dave Concepcion 5	Andruw Jones 9

[7] Joe Morgan and Bobby Richardson.
[8] Buddy Bell, Eric Chavez, and Robin Ventura.

CHAPTER 6
STADIUMS

Ninety feet between bases is perhaps as close as man has ever come to perfection.

—Red Smith, Hall-of-Fame writer

UNIQUE FIELDS

Old ballparks were weird, and so were the *ground rules*. At Comiskey Park in Chicago, the foul lines were old water hoses that had been squished flat and painted white. At Cleveland Stadium, the groundskeepers kept their tools in foul territory. (Until 1954, players throughout the majors were allowed to leave their gloves on the field after the third out.) Seals Stadium in San Francisco had no warning track. Municipal Stadium in Kansas City, Missouri, had a device buried in the ground that blew compressed air on home plate so the umpire wouldn't have to bend over and brush the dirt away. At Huntington Avenue Baseball Grounds in Boston, the outfield wall measured just 280 feet down the right-field line and more than 600 feet to center.

Nowadays, every ballpark has a warning track and chalk foul lines, the groundskeepers have entire rooms under the stands for their equipment, and you'll never see extreme distances to outfield walls; all parks built after 1957 had to be at least 325 feet down the lines and 400 feet to center. But there's no rule about the shape and height of outfield walls or the amount of foul territory. Every field is different, and that's one of the many things that sets baseball apart from most other sports. Tennis courts are always 78 feet long. Football fields are always 160 feet wide. North American hockey rinks are all the same size. Basketball courts? Identical. Of course, certain measurements on a baseball diamond must be uniform, such as the distance between bases (90 feet) and from home plate to the pitching rubber (60 feet, 6 inches), the size of the batter's boxes (4-by-6 feet), the diameter of the mound (18 feet), and the distance from home to second base (127 feet, 3⅜ inches).

Despite these fixed measurements, many ballparks still have distinctive features and personalities. Here are the top 10.

FENWAY PARK, BOSTON Baseball's oldest stadium opened on April 20, 1912—the same week the *Titanic* sank. Fenway's most famous feature is the 37-foot wall in left field that became known in 1947 as the Green Monster when a coating of green paint (later copyrighted as "Fenway Green") covered its original advertisements. The Monster, which measures just 310 feet down the line and displays the initials of former owners Tom and Jean Yawkey in Morse code, is both a blessing and a curse for a batter: it turns many routine fly balls into extra-base hits, but can mess up a hitter's swing if he tries to hit everything in that direction. (When Bill "Spaceman" Lee, a former Red Sox pitcher, saw the Monster for the first time, he said, "Do they leave it there during the game?") In right field, the *foul pole* is called the Pesky Pole because of a former Red Sox infielder named Johnny Pesky, who wrapped several balls just inside of it for important home runs in the late 1940s. It stands just 302 feet from home plate, but the right-field wall juts back sharply to a distance of 380 feet.

WRIGLEY FIELD, CHICAGO The home of the Cubs, baseball's second oldest stadium features ivy-covered outfield walls and Bleacher Bums, the rowdy fans who started the popular tradition of throwing opposing players' *gopher balls* back onto the field. They had many chances on May 17, 1979, when Wrigley's famous wind was blowing in their direction and helped produce 11 home runs in a 23–22 *slugfest* that lasted 10 innings. Wrigley, which in 1988 became the last major league ballpark to add lights for night baseball, is so small that home runs regularly land outside of it on Waveland and Sheffield Avenues, where fans known as Ballhawks battle for the prized souvenirs.

YANKEE STADIUM, NEW YORK Babe Ruth drew so many fans when the Yankees acquired him that the team's owners could afford to build baseball's first triple-decked stadium. It opened in 1923 and quickly became known as "The House That Ruth Built." During renovations in the 1970s, MLB allowed the Yankees to keep the famous *short porch* in right field because the ballpark had been constructed before 1957. In 1961 Roger Maris's record-breaking 61st home run of the season (which bested Ruth's long-standing total of 60) landed there, but it wouldn't have left most other parks.

MCAFEE COLISEUM, OAKLAND Home of baseball's first appearance of "The Wave" in 1981, the Coliseum has so much foul territory that it reduces batting averages by five to seven points (because fielders have more room to chase foul pop-ups). No hometown player has ever won a *batting title,* though third baseman Carney Lansford came close in 1989 when his .336 average left him three points short of Twins Hall-of-Fame center fielder Kirby Puckett. The Coliseum (or "Mausoleum," as it's been called because of its huge, uninviting concrete structure) is also home to the NFL's Oakland Raiders. When the upper deck was permanently closed for baseball before the 2006 season in order to create a more intimate and cozy vibe, the seating capacity dropped to 34,179, the lowest in the majors.

COORS FIELD, DENVER All the seats are dark blue except for one purple row in the upper deck, which is exactly one mile above sea level. Because of the high altitude, the air is thin and provides less resistance; thus, pitchers don't get as much movement, and fly balls travel 9 percent farther. To compensate, Coors has deep fences, and the Rockies store their baseballs in a humidor to keep them from drying out—but the ballpark is still a hitter's paradise. In 1999 the Rockies and their opponents hit 303 home runs, the most in one season at one venue.

MINUTE MAID PARK, HOUSTON At 436 feet, the Major Leagues' deepest wall belongs to the Astros, but the shallow *alleys* and short porch in left field make it easy to hit home runs. (The stadium, originally named Enron Field, was nicknamed "Tenrun Field" because of the many high-scoring games.) Just in front of the center-field wall, there's a hill and a flagpole in play. Some old ballparks had similar obstacles, but there's nothing else like it today.

ORIOLE PARK AT CAMDEN YARDS, BALTIMORE This is another hitter-friendly ballpark, but being two blocks from Babe Ruth's birthplace has nothing to do with it; home runs fly out because it's a *bandbox*. The right-field backdrop features the Baltimore & Ohio Warehouse, the longest building on the East Coast at 1,016 feet.

COMERICA PARK, DETROIT This stadium was built larger than necessary. When the Tigers moved there in 2000, the *front office* couldn't convince power hitters to sign with the team until the fences were moved in. So much for being pitcher-friendly.

THE METRODOME, MINNEAPOLIS At its highest point, the roof is only 195 feet above the field. Many balls hit it and stay in play, but two never came down: in 1984, A's designated hitter Dave Kingman launched a *major league pop-up* into a drainage valve, and in 1996, Indians infielder Alvaro Espinoza lifted one that got stuck in a speaker.[1] Both players were awarded doubles. The Twins' ballpark has had several nicknames, including "Homerdome" because of the many home runs and "Thunderdome" because of how loud crowd noises can get. During the 1987 postseason, experts compared the decibel level to that of a jet airplane taking off.

AT&T PARK, SAN FRANCISCO Because the architects had to squeeze the stadium into a small piece of land between a major boulevard and the bay, they designed a 24-foot wall in right field to compensate for the short distance—309 feet— from home plate to the foul pole (and to honor Giants outfielder Willie Mays, who wore uniform number 24). Many homers in that direction clear the stadium entirely; those

---

[1] Four other players have hit balls that defied gravity. Rupert Jones (1979) and Ricky Nelson (1983) got help from speakers at the Kingdome. Jose Canseco (1999) and Kevin Millar (2002) can thank the catwalks at Tampa's Tropicana Field.

that land in the water (named McCovey Cove for Willie McCovey, a Hall-of-Fame first baseman who played the majority of his career for the Giants in the 1960s and 1970s) are called "splash hits." Competition for the balls is fierce. Some fans hurl nets from the promenade, while others patrol the bay in kayaks and, occasionally, wet suits.

GROUNDSKEEPERS

How do you stop the other team's running game? You need a pitcher with a quick delivery, a catcher with a *gun*, and a few bold groundskeepers.

Groundskeepers?

Yup. They might "accidentally" water the infield dirt too much and (whoops!) drop some sand to prevent a speedster from getting good footing. In the 1960s, the groundskeepers at San Francisco's Candlestick Park regularly used these tricks when the Dodgers came to town with Maury Wills, their speedy shortstop, and the base path between first and second earned a nickname: Maury's Lake. On the other hand, the speedy Angels of the 1970s gained a slight base-stealing edge at home after second base was secretly moved several inches closer to first.

Tricks like these are sneaky but not necessarily illegal because both teams face the same conditions. Other examples? If the home team's pitching staff has a couple of sinkerballers, the grounds crew can slow the visitors' grounders by growing the grass long. Or if the home team loves to bunt, the groundskeepers can help keep slow rollers in fair territory by making sure there's no slope along the infield foul lines and putting down a thick layer of chalk. Because the slope often varies from one stadium to the next, visiting players—especially the third baseman and anyone who loves to bunt—always roll a few balls down the lines during practice to see which way they go.

Some home-field advantages go too far. In 1965 the Mets accused the groundskeepers at Houston's Astrodome of manipulating the air-conditioning system to create air currents that hindered their fly balls and helped those hit by the Astros. Years later, visiting players in Minnesota made a similar complaint. The Twins denied it, but a former Metrodome employee eventually admitted that he had tampered with the dome's air flow by turning powerful electric fans on and off at strategic points late in games.

All groundskeepers—honest and otherwise—work so hard to repair the field's surface and appearance that they struggle to find enough time to eat dinner after the game's first pitch. Here are some things they do:

- They mow lanes and patterns in the grass by driving the mower in different directions. (The mower, in addition to cutting the grass, also presses it flat.)

- They paint the pitching rubber and home plate.

- Using a heavy tool called a tamp, they pound and harden the dirt around home plate and in front of the rubber.

- They set up and remove protective screens for batting practice.

- They water the infield dirt so it stays moist and soft—but not too soft or the players will leave footprints, which cause bad hops.

- They smooth the infield dirt by dragging it every few innings, even in extra innings.

- They replace dirty bases with fresh ones, then scrub and paint the old ones so they can be used again.

- They run onto the field between innings and pick up trash that blows out of the stands.

- They monitor the weather and frantically cover the field with the tarpaulin when it starts raining.

- After a rain delay, they sprinkle the right amount of *Turface* or *Diamond Dust*—special sandlike materials that are used to absorb water—on the muddy spots and rake it in.

And the next day they do all of it all over again.

ASTROTURF

The Astrodome (which closed after the 1999 season) originally had a roof with glass panels and a field with real grass. But the glass created a glare, and the fielders couldn't see the ball. Some of the panels were then painted white, but this blocked the sunlight and killed the grass. The Astros needed a solution and came up with ChemGrass, a synthetic playing surface first used on April 8, 1966, against the Dodgers. Soon after, ChemGrass became known as AstroTurf.

NASA sent men to the moon three years later, and *Star Wars* hit theaters less than a decade after that. People were obsessed with sleek, futuristic stuff, and AstroTurf was baseball's contribution. New ballparks at the time (like Three Rivers Stadium in Pittsburgh and Veterans Stadium in Philadelphia, both of which have already closed) were ugly for many reasons. Fake grass was one of them. But owners loved the *carpet* because it was cheaper and easier to maintain, especially in multipurpose facilities where the National Football League also played.

The players hated AstroTurf. Not only did it bake under the summer sun and make the fields unbearably hot, but it had no give. It wore down their bodies and hurt when they dove on it. (That's an understatement.) After all, it was just a thin layer of bristly green material on top of concrete. It also changed the game; average grounders became *seeing-eye singles,* and average line drives scooted past outfielders for extra-base hits. Okay, so there were fewer bad hops—but bad hops are part of baseball's charm.

Owners finally realized that AstroTurf was lame. Several teams ditched it in the 1990s, and new domes have since been built with retractable roofs and natural playing surfaces. The 2004 Blue Jays were the last team to play on AstroTurf; the following season they switched to FieldTurf, a synthetic surface made to look like real grass. (It doesn't.) The Devil Rays (FieldTurf) and the Twins (AstroPlay) are the only other teams still stuck with fields that everyone hates.

THE SUN

In the late afternoon, someone on the field always has the misfortune of facing west and looking right into the setting sun. Ever notice that it's usually the right fielder? (Better he should suffer than the batter.) That's because most ballparks, at the suggestion of baseball's rule book, face east-northeast if you're looking at the pitcher's mound from home plate.

Several stadiums face due east, while a few face southeast and others face due north. Minute Maid Park is the only stadium with any westward orientation—slightly west of north—but the Texas sun rarely affects the games; it's so hot that team officials often close the stadium's retractable roof during daylight hours.

WELCOME TO [INSERT UGLY NAME HERE] FIELD

Ballparks used to have nice, sensible names. Tiger Stadium in Detroit was named after the Tigers. The Baker Bowl in Philadelphia was named after Phillies owner William F. Baker. Jarry Park in Montreal was named after Jarry Street, which passed behind the left-field bleachers.

Now, in addition to the hideous names you've read earlier in this chapter, there are places like Safeco Field in Seattle, U.S. Cellular Field in Chicago, and Citizens Bank Park in Philadelphia. That's because huge corporations pay millions of dollars for the naming rights. Even the seemingly wholesome and patriotic name of the Reds' new stadium, Great American Ball Park, was bought by an insurance company called—you guessed it—Great American.

Thankfully, not all the owners are selling out, but can you blame the ones who do? When the Mets move into their new home in 2009, Citigroup Inc. will start paying the team an estimated $20 million a year through 2028 to call it Citi Field.

BALLPARK DIAGRAMS

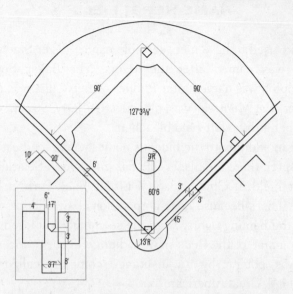

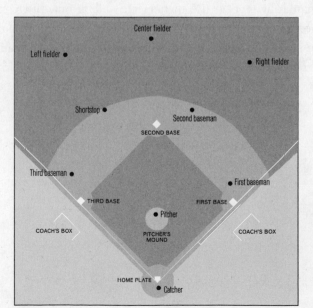

CHAPTER 7
UMPIRES

We're supposed to be perfect our first day on the job and then show constant improvement.

—Ed Vargo, former major league umpire

TOUGH JOB

You knew early on that you weren't quite good enough to make it as a player. And now you realize that you pretty much had to have been a player if you ever wanted to coach or grace the broadcasters' booth. But you *have to* make it. It's been your lifelong dream. You must find some way to get out there on that field with those guys. Deep inside, you're one of them. The ballpark is home. It's where you belong. You were born for this game.

You could be a trainer, but medical school and blood and guts isn't your thing. You could be a batboy, but you're looking for more than a summer fling, and besides, you're not the owner's ex-wife's half-brother's friend's 13-year-old nephew. You could be a groundskeeper, but you saw enough grass in college.

Not too many options left—looks like you're gonna be an umpire. Okay, you can deal with that. You know the strike zone. You can handle a *double switch*. You work well under pressure. Infield fly rule? Piece-a-cake.

You buy yourself a rule book and a mask and volunteer to work the plate at Little League games. You realize that calling strike three is fun. The kids are adorable when they throw tantrums, and their parents are amusingly predictable when they insult you—they're just bitter that their kid is playing right field and batting ninth. And when the coaches barrel onto the field to argue, you feel more alive than ever. Hell yeah, you could do this for a while, and you decide to go for it.

You do a little research online and make some phone calls. You hop a flight to Florida and throw down a couple thousand bucks for a five-week session at umpire school. Your friends think you're outta your head. You don't care. You learn weird rules. You learn proper stances and positioning. You learn voice control. You learn how to tame future Hall of Famers who scream in your face and tell you how worthless you are. You log 300 hours in the field. You pass your tests and graduate as one of the best in your class. The school's instructors, along with staff members of the Professional Baseball Umpire Corporation, select you and a few others to participate in an official Umpire Evaluation Course. As one of the best, you get recommended to the minor league presidents.

You say good-bye to your family and hello to $1,800 per month as you head off for a career in pro baseball. Like the players, you live off fast food, endure endless road trips, and stay at the cheapest hotels. And this is just the first few weeks.

Most minor league umpires have to wait at least eight years before being considered for a promotion to the majors. It's been 12 years for you and still no word. You're tired. You're depressed. You can barely support your family. You know the ball boys better than you know your own children.

You finish your 13th minor league season. At least you've been in Triple-A for the last few years, but it's the same story: no promotion. You're almost ready to quit, but your friends talk you out of it. You go back for a 14th season, unsure of how much longer you can go on. And then, one day around the *All-Star break* . . .

. . . you get the call! Congratulations, you've finally made it to The Show. Now everyone hates you. The fans don't pay to watch you. They don't even want to know you exist, and they'll remind you of it each time you make a close call that doesn't go their way, even if you're right, and you usually are. After all, you've learned to watch the runner's foot hit the bag while listening for the ball hitting the first baseman's glove. You've been trained to let the shortstop get away with some fancy footwork on the neighborhood play—but not too much. You know how to handle interference, obstruction, appeals, and substitutions. You act confident and stand firm in your decisions.

You're now earning well over six figures, but your ego takes a daily beating. Aside from the abuse from players, coaches, managers, and fans, the announcers second-guess every one of your close calls while watching slow-motion replays from five different angles. And *still,* they can't always tell if the guy is safe or out.

The strike zone, previously open to slight interpretation, has gotten strict. Major League Baseball officials want consistency and have begun using an electronic system called QuesTec to evaluate your balls and strikes. But the technology, which relies on cameras in the stands and on the dugouts, isn't installed in all the ballparks. Even worse, every ballpark is different, and the machines are operated by error-prone human beings, not unlike you. There's a serious lack of consistency, scary considering that if your calls fail to match

QuesTec at least 90 percent of the time, the league could take disciplinary action. Your livelihood now depends on judgment calls that are beyond your control.

And hey, how's your shoulder been feeling since that 97-mph foul tip caught a piece of you last week?

THE FAIR BALL QUIZ

You still think you have what it takes to be a big league umpire? Then grab a piece of paper and take the Fair Ball Quiz to test your knowledge of the rule book. Write "fair" or "foul" for each of the following situations. You'll find the answers and explanations at the end of this chapter.

1. A fly ball hits the foul pole.

2. A deep fly ball lands in fair territory, then bounces over the wall on the foul side of the foul pole.

3. A fly ball lands on a pebble in foul territory and bounces into fair territory.

4. A bunt rolls onto home plate and stays there.

5. The third baseman lets a bunt roll foul, but he reaches across the foul line and touches it while standing in fair territory.

6. A line drive sails above first base in fair territory, then hooks and lands foul down the right-field line.

7. A grounder bounces past first base in fair territory, then hooks and rolls foul before reaching the foul pole.

8. A grounder touches fair territory, then bounces directly over first base and lands in foul territory.

9. A line drive up the middle hits the pitching rubber and ricochets into foul territory between third and home.

10. A line drive up the middle hits the pitcher's shoe and ricochets into foul territory between first and home.

11. A pop-up drifts past the edge of the stands into foul territory, then gets blown back by the wind and lands in fair territory.

THE STRIKE ZONE

Most fans have a general concept of the strike zone. They know it's over the plate and between the hitter's knees and his chest. Or is it his armpits? Or his shoulders? Or no, wait, it's the letters on the front of his uniform?

It's definitely not the uniform. If letters marked the top of the zone, teams would sew their names onto their belts.

The strike zone is determined after the batter gets into his stance; the more he crouches, the smaller the pitcher's target. The hollow beneath his kneecaps then marks the bottom of the zone, while the top of the zone is halfway between his belt and the top of his shoulders. (In case you're wondering, there's no rule that prevents the hitter from wearing his belt—or his pants, for that matter—around his ankles.)

Of course, this is just the rule-book definition of the strike zone. Out on the field, every ump's zone varies slightly. After all, they're human. But if that's not a good enough excuse, consider that the ump has to choose which of the catcher's shoulders to look over, and that affects his ability to judge pitches on the other side of the strike zone. One ump might give an extra inch or two off the outside corner. Another might not call high strikes. The players don't care as long as each ump is consistent for both teams. That way, they can adjust their approach. If the leadoff hitter gets *rung up* on a borderline pitch, he might return to the dugout and tell his teammates, "He's callin' it today, fellas." Meanwhile, the relief pitchers might be studying the ump's strike zone by watching the game on a TV in the clubhouse.

"YER OUTTA HERE!"

An umpire communicates his decisions by using the following gestures:

- **Safe**—He flings his arms out to each side with his palms down.

- **Out**—He pumps his fist.

- **Ball**—He makes no gesture, but often says "ball" so the hitter and catcher know the call.

- **Strike**—He points (sometimes with one or two fingers, depending on the count) or punches to the side.

- **Foul tip**—He extends one arm and swipes the top of it several times with his other hand moving away from his body. Then he makes a "strike" gesture.

- **Hit by pitch**—He points at first base.

- **Time-out**—He extends his arms over his head. (If the catcher requests time out, the ump points at him to let the pitcher know.)

- **Time-in**—The home-plate umpire points at the pitcher.

- **Fair/foul ball**—On a grounder that doesn't reach first or third base, the home-plate ump rules "fair" by pointing toward fair territory or "foul" by using the "time-out" gesture. Otherwise, the first- or third-base ump makes the call by pointing in the appropriate direction. (An umpire doesn't make any gesture if the ball clearly rolls or lands foul.)

- **Home run**—He raises his arm and makes a circular motion at the wrist with his index finger pointing up, as if to say, "Circle the bases."

- *Ground-rule double*—He holds up two fingers.

- **Infield fly**—He reaches high, points up, and yells, "Infield fly!"

- **Fan interference**—If a fan reaches over the wall and touches a ball that's in play, the ump lifts both hands over his head and grabs his wrist. (If the ball was hit, the batter automatically gets a double. If the ball was thrown, all runners get to advance one base if the pitcher threw it while touching the rubber and two bases for any other throw.) If a fan reaches over the wall but doesn't touch the ball, the ump uses the "safe" gesture to indicate that it's still in play.

- **No catch**—When a fielder *traps* the ball, meaning he catches it a fraction of a second after it hits the ground, the ump uses the "safe" gesture.

- **No pitch**—Occasionally, when the ump awards the batter's time-out request at the last second, the pitcher doesn't notice and still goes into his windup. As the ump bolts out of the way, he waves his arms over his head— in the motion of a "safe" call—to try to get the pitcher's attention and to indicate that the pitch does not count.

- **Possession/no possession**—If a throw beats the runner on a force play but the fielder briefly bobbles the ball, the ump calls "safe" and follows with a juggling gesture. If the fielder catches the ball but drops it while taking it out of his glove, the ump calls "out" and then mimes removing the ball from the glove. (This call is made most often at second base during a botched double play.)

- *Check swing*—The catcher points at whichever umpire has a better view (third base for left-handed hitters and first base for righties) to receive a ruling on whether the batter held up or swung past the front edge of home plate. The ump then calls a ball or strike by using the "safe" or "out" gesture.

- **Run scores**—If a runner touches home plate before the fielding team tags another runner for the third out, the ump points at the plate to indicate that the run counts.

- **Foot off the base**—If an errant throw pulls the fielder off the base on a force play, the ump flings both arms to one side with his palms out.

- **Balk**—Any umpire can make this call by pointing at the pitcher and yelling, "Balk!"

- **Pitching change**—It's the manager's decision, but the ump sometimes signals for him by raising his right or left arm (to indicate whether the manager wants a righty or lefty) and pointing toward the bullpen.

- **Substitution**—He calls time, looks up toward the public address announcer's booth behind home plate, and points at the replacement.

- **Warning**—When a *beanball* war prompts the home-plate umpire to warn both teams not to retaliate further, he takes a step toward each dugout and points at it, adding a brief verbal explanation so the managers understand the situation.

- **Ejection**—Any ump can eject a player or coach[1] by pointing his index finger and flinging his hand forward (as if he's throwing a ball) and, of course, yelling, "Yer outta here!"

BORDERLINE CALLS

We like to think that umpires don't hold grudges. Obviously, if a runner gets thrown out at first base by two steps, the ump won't call the guy "safe" just because the first baseman called him fat nine years ago after a flubbed pick-off call. But an ump remembers things like that and might consider them later on when making borderline calls.

Think about how difficult it can be for the home-plate umpire to choose "ball" or "strike." Did that backdoor slider *paint the corner?* Did it stay half an inch outside? The call can go either way. But which way? Someone's going to be angry. Who should it be? The ump might base his decision on the reputation of the players involved. That's why a catcher shouldn't argue during his at-bats; his bad attitude could be used against him and his pitcher when his team returns to the field.

The players' experience can also be a factor. If a rookie pitcher faces a batter with 1,500 career walks, guess who gets

---

[1]Players and coaches aren't the only ones who can get the boot. In 1985 a minor league organist was ejected by the home-plate ump for playing "Three Blind Mice" after what he thought was a bad call against the home team.

the benefit of the doubt. Ted Williams, known for his acute vision and extraordinary knowledge of the strike zone, was once batting when a young catcher complained about a close pitch that was called a ball. "Son," replied the ump, "when the pitch is a strike, Mr. Williams will let you know."

ARGUING

Football, basketball, and hockey use the *instant replay,* but baseball doesn't (except for that one time in 1999 when a 28-year umpire named Frank Pulli buckled under pressure from both teams and used TV replays to determine that Cliff Floyd's deep line drive against the Cardinals at Dolphins Stadium had in fact not cleared the outfield wall). As a result, the only time an umpire reverses his decision is when another ump has a better view and is sure he saw the play differently. But this happens so rarely that you might wonder why a manager even bothers to argue.

First, he needs to protect his players. Longtime Orioles manager Earl Weaver said, "The job of arguing with the umpire belongs to the manager because it won't hurt the team if he gets thrown out of the game."

In addition to protection, a manager can boost the spirit of a player who feels wronged by a bad call by continuing the argument on his behalf. He might even decide to get ejected to rev up his team; Weaver used to tell his players, "I'm outta here, boys," before climbing the dugout steps.

Even if the manager agrees with the ump, he can reap the benefits of a good argument—he'll still storm onto the field, flail his arms, kick dirt, throw his hat, and appear to curse a lot while actually saying something like "That was the *best* gosh-darn call I have ever seen! I cannot be-*lieve* what a great freakin' umpire you are!"

But most arguments are real and have more substance than:

"He was out!"

"He beat the tag!"

"No, he didn't!"

"Yes, he did!"

The manager might ask the ump to explain the play from his point of view. Or he could argue that the ump was out of position and unable to see it in the first place. Or he might complain that the ump is being inconsistent and only giving the call to the other guys. Regardless of the issue, he might earn consideration on a close play later in the game by making the ump feel guilty about possibly blowing a call.

Whether the dispute ends peacefully or as a dirt-kicking, saliva-flying, cooler-tipping tirade, the ump might get defensive. But deep down, he knows that the manager is doing his job by making a spectacle. Still, if the manager makes it personal and says the magic words, he'll be taking an early shower. (The magic words are not "please" and "thank you.")

RANDOM UMP STUFF

FOURSOMES Umpires travel in groups of four, and they rotate their positions each game. None of them wants to be behind the plate because it's stressful and physically draining, but even the *crew chief* has to do it.

PROFESSIONAL COURTESY When the home-plate umpire gets whacked by a foul tip, the catcher gives him time to recover by making a trip to the mound, even if he has nothing to say to his pitcher. When the catcher gets nailed, the ump returns the favor by brushing off the plate, even if there's no dirt on it.

I GOT YOUR BACK When the home-plate ump drops down into his pre-pitch stance, he sometimes reaches out and gently places one hand on the catcher's back to steady himself. Big leaguers are used to the contact, but it can be a bit distracting for younger catchers who are new to the position.

MUD If a brand-new ball went straight from its Rawlings box to the mound, the pitcher would struggle to grip its slick surface, and the whiteness of the ball would deflect light and create a glare for the hitters. To prevent this, umpires (or their assistants) rub mud on all the balls. But not any mud will do. All professional teams use the same kind: Lena Blackburne Rubbing Mud, named after Russell Aubrey "Lena" Blackburne, a former major league player and coach who discovered the substance in the 1930s. The mud's ingredients and location are top secret, though some people believe it's collected at low tide from a tributary of the Delaware River in southern New Jersey.

BALLS The home-plate umpire inspects every ball that hits the dirt. If it's still in good shape, he hands it back to the catcher or drops it into the ball pouch at his hip. If it's scuffed, a crafty pitcher would use the irregularity of the ball's surface to gain extra movement, so the ump removes it from play by rolling it to a ball boy near the home team's dugout.[2] When the ump's supply dwindles, he looks at the ball boy and holds up several fingers to indicate how many more he needs.

CORRECTION When the scoreboard operator messes up the count, the ump eliminates all confusion by holding up the

---

[2]The average major league baseball lasts just six pitches. The average team goes through 36,000 balls a year.

appropriate number of fingers. When you see him do it on TV, it'll look like he has it backwards. That's because the center-field camera is facing him while he flashes the count from his own perspective: balls with his left hand, strikes with his right.

MOVE IT! Once in a while, if you look carefully, you might see the batter pat the top of his helmet a few times. This is a secret way of asking the second-base umpire to move out of his line of vision.

STRIKE? After swinging at a borderline pitch for strike three, the hitter sometimes asks, "Hey, *blue,* would that've been a strike?" This is part of the process of learning each ump's strike zone.

HEY, FATSO Why are all umps fat? They're not. In fact, they're supposed to stay in shape so they can move quickly and see the action from the best possible angles. Watch how fast they run toward the outfielders on deep fly balls. And keep in mind that the home-plate ump wears a bulky chest protector under his clothes.

OBSTRUCTED VIEW If you're at the game and can't see the foul lines or outfield corners, look at the first- or third-base umpire as soon as a fly ball escapes your view. You'll see his call and be the first fan in your section to know if it's fair or foul.

NO CALL Sometimes a runner tries so hard to avoid being tagged at home plate that he misses the plate itself. But if he doesn't leave the baseline in the process, he's not out, even if he ends up near the backstop or starts walking toward the dugout. Of course, he's not safe either, so the play remains active and the ump doesn't make a call. (On occasion, you might see the runner scamper to avoid the catcher 20 feet from the plate.)

HIT BY A PITCH? If a pitch merely grazes a thread dangling off the hitter's jersey, it counts as a hit by pitch. But if the ump doesn't see it, there's no way to prove it happened. If, however, the hitter gets nicked on the foot and doesn't get the call, he's not necessarily out of luck. In Game 5 of the 1969 World Series, Cleon Jones got hit by Orioles left-hander Mike Cuellar and was denied first base—until Mets manager Gil Hodges retrieved the ball and showed the ump that it had a shoe-polish smudge.

CONFERENCES Because there's no delay-of-game penalty for a conference on the mound, the fielding team drags it out when one of its relievers is scrambling to get loose. Sure, the ump will break it up and try to keep things moving, but think about how much time it takes. First, the manager gives the "yap" sign, prompting the catcher to walk out to the mound (12 seconds) and shoot the breeze with his pitcher (16 seconds). Then the ump walks out (12 seconds) and says, "Okay, fellas, let's play ball" (2 seconds). He and the catcher jog back to the plate (6 seconds) and settle into their crouches (3 seconds). The pitcher steps onto the rubber (1 second) and looks at the signs for a pitch he'll never throw (3 seconds). Then he steps off (three-quarters of a second), and the manager slowly walks from the dugout to the mound (22 seconds), where he blabs to all the infielders about the free premium channels he has in his hotel room and what movies he's gonna watch after the game (17 seconds). The ump briskly walks back to the mound (9 seconds) and says, "What's it gonna be, boys?" (2 seconds). The manager tells him that he's gonna go with his *southpaw*

(3 seconds) and asks about the wife and kids (1 second). The ump says they're fine (half a second) and signals to the bullpen (three-quarters of a second). That's an extra minute and 51 seconds for the guy getting loose—and he still gets to throw eight warm-up pitches when he takes the mound.

VISITATION RIGHTS The second time a manager or coach visits the pitcher in one inning, even if it's a different coach each time, he must remove the pitcher from the game. When the trainer heads to the mound, the ump joins him to make sure that the only thing being discussed is the pitcher's health. Otherwise, the trainer could relay instructions from a coach without the team being charged for one of its two visits.

ANSWERS TO THE FAIR BALL QUIZ

If you've been flipping through this book in no particular order and stumbled upon this section, don't read it. It contains the answers to the Fair Ball Quiz on page 116. Take the quiz. Then come back.

1. Fair ball and a home run. (Why don't they call it the fair pole?)

2. Fair. The foul pole means nothing unless the ball reaches it on a fly.

3. Foul. It doesn't matter where a fly ball bounces, only where it lands.

4. Fair. The plate is part of fair territory.

5. Foul. The location of the ball is the only thing that matters.

6. Foul. If the ball is in the air, it doesn't matter where it passes the base.

7. Fair. A grounder simply has to pass the base in fair territory. Then it can roll anywhere.

8. Fair. It doesn't have to land past the base in fair territory.

9. Foul. The rubber is part of the field, and the ball didn't pass the base in fair territory.

10. Fair. Whether he caught it, kicked it, or kissed it, the ball was fair when he touched it.

11. Fair. The ball is out of play only if it lands there.

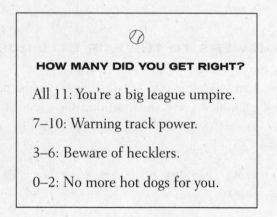

HOW MANY DID YOU GET RIGHT?

All 11: You're a big league umpire.

7–10: Warning track power.

3–6: Beware of hecklers.

0–2: No more hot dogs for you.

CHAPTER 8
STATISTICS

⚾

During my 18 years I came to bat almost 10,000 times. I struck out about 1,700 times and walked maybe 1,800 times. You figure a ballplayer will average about 500 at-bats a season. That means I played seven years without ever hitting the ball.

—Mickey Mantle, Hall-of-Fame outfielder

THE NUMBERS GAME

Averages. Percentages. Ratios. Totals.

Players produce them. Scoreboards display them. Managers analyze them. Writers report them. Historians document them. Baseball cards feature them. Fans memorize them. Salaries are based on them.

While baseball has always embraced statistics, the numbers craze began in the early 1980s when a die-hard fan and mathematician named Bill James started interpreting and publishing lists of stats. Within a few years, his reports became best-sellers and revolutionized the statistical analysis of Major League Baseball. In 2002 Red Sox president Larry Lucchino hired James as a "baseball-performance evaluator and predictor."

Nowadays, there's a stat for everything. While a manager needs to know which of his players has the best batting average after the seventh inning with less than two outs and runners in scoring position when facing a lefty on artificial turf in a day game after a night game in June, the opposing manager needs to know which of his relief pitchers is most likely to strike that player out.

STAT HISTORY

Many people think baseball is perfect. They believe that the distance to the pitcher's mound and from home to first—along with the angles, the shapes, the lines, the rules, and the size of the ball—could not have been designed better. But it took a century to get everything right. In the earliest days of professional baseball, the unrefined rules governed a much different game whose simple statistics were poorly recorded. Here are some ways the sport has evolved.

1850S Since electricity hadn't been invented, there was no night baseball. Games ended when it got dark, so the winning teams were known to stall. The umpire would call a strike only after warning the batter for intentionally delaying the game by refusing to swing at good pitches. The ball was slightly larger, and the batter was out if the fielding team caught his hit on one bounce.

1860S The foul lines were invented, players couldn't be substituted after the third inning unless there was an injury, and the umpire would call a ball only after warning the pitcher for intentionally delaying the game by throwing bad pitches.

1870S The home team batted first, hitters were allowed to request a high or low pitch, and the umpire—there was only one for each game—could ask the spectators for help if he missed seeing a play.

1880S The number of balls required for a walk was gradually reduced from nine to four, a strikeout changed from four strikes to three, and batters were awarded first base if hit by a pitch.

In 1893 the distance from the pitcher's mound to home plate increased from 50 feet to its current distance of 60 feet, 6 inches. Clearly, the adjustment favored the hitters and affected the statistics of all players. Though many other rules have come and gone, this was the most significant, and it marks the beginning of baseball's *modern era*.

Here are some modern, stat-altering changes:

1898—Stolen bases were no longer awarded for all daring baserunning maneuvers, such as tagging up or making it from first to third on a single.

1901—The National League started counting foul balls as strikes. This reduced scoring by 12 percent.

1903—The American League adopted the foul-strike rule, and strikeouts increased by 58 percent.

1911—The cork-centered baseball was introduced and brought more offense with it.

1920—*Walk-off home runs* were finally counted as home runs instead of the smallest hit necessary to push across the winning run. (Babe Ruth's career total would have been 715 instead of 714 had this rule been around sooner.)

1950—The pitcher's mound had to be exactly 15 inches high.

1961—The regular season was extended from 154 to 162 games.

1969—Saves became an official stat, and the mound was lowered to 10 inches.

1973—Hello, designated hitter.[1]

1998—Major League Baseball expanded to its current total of 30 teams with the addition of the Devil Rays and Diamondbacks. This weakened the overall level of play—and helped the superstars achieve even greater success—by creating 50 openings for players who would've (and should've) been in the minors.

2004—MLB began penalizing players for using steroids.

Modern statisticians have debated whether to use current rules to adjust earlier statistics that were calculated differently. Batting averages, for example, were skewed when walks counted as hits in 1876 and as outs in 1887. In general, statisticians have agreed on minor adjustments to certain numbers but have avoided stripping players of awards and titles years after they earned them.

Baseball's evolution makes it difficult to compare players from different eras. Sure, a .300 batting average has long been the mark of excellence (maybe it should be .310 for lefties because they stand on the first-base side of home plate and automatically get a two-step head start), but other accomplishments must now be judged differently. Some people think that Bob Gibson's 1968 season, in which he recorded a microscopic 1.12 earned run average, is the most dominant ever for a

---

[1]Important piece of trivia: on April 6, 1973, Ron Blomberg of the Yankees became the first DH.

pitcher. Other people, however, are more impressed with Greg Maddux's 1994 season, even though his ERA was 1.54. That's because he was 2.65 runs below the National League's season average of 4.21, whereas Gibson finished 1.87 runs below the average of 2.99. In addition, the mound was five inches higher in 1968, giving pitchers extra leverage and such a huge advantage that it was lowered the following season.

Home run totals are also hard to compare because players keep slugging more and more of them. Why? Because today's hitters lift weights and play in smaller ballparks. Because lots of guys are allegedly using steroids. Because the baseballs are wound tighter and travel farther. Because the umpires' reluctance to call strikes on letter-high pitches has shrunk the strike zone. Because *expansion* has thinned pitching talent. Sadly, the once exclusive 500 home run club now welcomes a new member every year or two.

Fans have a lot to consider when arguing about the greatest home run hitter of all time. Is it Babe Ruth? He pioneered the *longball* and broke his own single-season record by hitting 60 home runs in 1927. Or Roger Maris? He surpassed Ruth's total 34 years later, but his record-breaking 61st blast came on the last day of the new 162-game schedule and forever had an *asterisk* attached to it. Or maybe it's Mark McGwire? He reached 500 home runs in the fewest number of at-bats and on his way to a new record of 70 in 1998 eclipsed Maris in his team's 144th game of the season—but the asterisk remained because he was involved in a steroid controversy. What about Barry Bonds? In 2001 he hit three more home runs than McGwire, but inherited the asterisk for the same reason. Perhaps it's Hank Aaron? He never hit more than 47 *roundtrippers* in a season but holds the career record with 755. Could it be Saduharu Oh? He never played in the majors, but hit 868 home runs in Japan, a world record for professional baseball.

While home run records have been repeatedly reestablished, other milestones have become harder to achieve. Consider the 20-win season for a pitcher. It's been an impressive accomplishment for almost a century, but fewer guys are doing it because teams shifted from four- to five-man *rotations* during the 1980s to preserve their pitchers' million-dollar arms. As a result, starters have fewer chances to win because they appear in fewer games. Here are some other hard-to-reach numbers:

- Cy Young pitched 749 complete games during his career. His record is safe because it would now take a pitcher more than 21 seasons just to start that many games.

- Fewer complete games means fewer shutouts. Walter Johnson's career record of 110 is untouchable.

- We probably won't ever see another 30-game winner. Denny McLain was the last pitcher to reach the mark with his 31-6 record in 1968. (Yeah, 1968.)

- In today's smaller ballparks, gappers get tracked down quicker by the outfielders; there's no way to break Chief Wilson's single-season record of 36 triples or Sam Crawford's career record of 309.

What other records are out of reach? Which ones are ready to fall? Turn to page 238, take a look at the lists of stats in appendix A, and decide for yourself.

MATH IS FUN

Get your calculator. It's time to learn about some important statistics.

ON-BASE PERCENTAGE (OBP) How often does the batter reach base? (This is the trickiest statistic to calculate, so let's get it out of the way first.) Add the player's hits, walks, and times hit by a pitch. Write that number and keep it separate. Now figure out a second number by adding his at-bats, walks, times hit by a pitch, and sacrifice flies. Write this new number after the first number and stick a division sign in the middle. That'll give you his on-base percentage. (Anything above .400 is fantastic.) Here's the formula: $(H + BB + HP) \div (AB + BB + HP + SF)$.

Let's practice the math on Barry Bonds, who holds the single-season OBP record at .609 (meaning he reached base nearly 61 percent of the time). Bonds achieved his astounding percentage in 2004 by collecting 135 hits, drawing a record 232 walks, getting hit by nine pitches, and stroking three sacrifice flies in 373 at-bats. Add the hits and walks to the number of times he was *beaned* and you get 376. Now add his at-bats, walks, hit by pitches, and sac flies and you get 617. Divide 376 by 617 and you're left with .60940032415, which rounds down to the more digestible .609. It gets easier from here.

SLUGGING PERCENTAGE (SLG) How good is the batter at delivering extra-base hits? Divide his *total bases* by his at-bats. (Total bases are the number of bases resulting in hits; a single is one base, a double is two, and so on.) The simple formula is $TB \div AB$, but first you might have to do some arithmetic to figure out the number of total bases.

Babe Ruth holds the career SLG record at .690. In 8,399 at-bats, he had 1,517 singles, 506 doubles, 136 triples, and 714 home runs. Add the number of bases from each (1,517 + 1,012 + 408 + 2,856) and you get 5,793 total bases. Divide that by 8,399 and there it is: .68972496725, which rounds up to .690. How impressive is that? Anything above .500 is good. A slugging percentage over .550 is great, and only a few players each season manage to break .600.

Now that you know both OBP and SLG, you can appreciate the batter's OPS—a popular stat these days that stands for "on-base plus slugging." Generally, these percentages will already be calculated for you, but you'll impress people if you understand how they work. Most fans have no clue.

STOLEN BASE PERCENTAGE (SB%) How often does the runner succeed when he tries to steal? Divide his stolen bases by total number of stolen base attempts (stolen bases plus times caught stealing). The formula: SB ÷ (SB + CS).

Enough with the record holders. Cecil Fielder, a hefty slugger who enjoyed his best years with the Tigers in the early 1990s, stole a total of two bases in 13 major league seasons. Unfortunately, he was caught stealing six times, so he succeeded twice in eight attempts. Two divided by eight equals .250, which means Fielder stole successfully just one-quarter of the time.

WINNING PERCENTAGE (PCT) How often does the team or pitcher or manager win? Divide wins by the number of wins and losses. The formula: W ÷ (W + L).

The 1899 Cleveland Spiders were the worst team in baseball history, finishing with 20 wins and 134 losses. (That's because the owners also bought the St. Louis franchise and transferred most of their stars that way, including Cy Young.) Add the wins and losses and you get 154. Divide 20 by 154, and you have a "winning" percentage of .130.

FIELDING AVERAGE (FA) How often does the fielder complete his plays without messing up? Add his *putouts* and *assists* and divide that number by his *total chances* (putouts + assists + errors). The formula: (PO + A) ÷ TC.

Ozzie Smith made 25 errors as a rookie with the 1978 Padres while recording 264 putouts and 548 assists. Add 264 to 548 and you get 812. Divide that number by 837—his total chances—and you'll see that the Wizard of Oz had a respectable .970 average.

Batting average and earned run average are so important that they have their own sections in this book. Keep reading.

BATTING AVERAGE

Batting average (AVG) is calculated by dividing hits by at-bats. The difficult part of this simple equation is knowing what counts as a hit and what counts as an at-bat. This section explains it.

It's Opening Day. Your favorite player comes to bat for the first time and rips a line drive up the middle. Base hit. He's 1-for-1 and *batting a thousand* because his average, always calculated to the third decimal place, currently equals 1.000.

In his second at-bat, he pops out to the catcher. Now 1-for-2, his average drops to .500 (or "five hundred").

On his next trip to the plate, he smacks a fair ball into the right-field corner, motors around the bases, and gets thrown out at third. He still gets credited with a double for having reached second base, so he's 2-for-3, and his batting average rounds up from .6666666666666666666 (etc.) to .667 (or "six sixty-seven").

His fourth time up, he walks. It's not a hit or an out, so both his batting average and total number of at-bats stay the same. That's why there's a statistic called plate appearances.

The announcer can say that the hitter is 2-for-3 and has reached base in three of four plate appearances.

In the ninth inning, he reaches first base when his routine grounder trickles through the shortstop's legs for an error. He should've been out, and his stats show it: at 2-for-4, he's back to .500.

On the second day of the season, he starts the game by looking at ball four. Overall, he's 2-for-4 with two walks.

With one out and a runner on first, he's up again and grounds into an inning-ending double play. He doesn't get penalized for both outs, but at 2-for-5, he does drop to .400.

He strikes out in his second at-bat. Now 2-for-6 on the young season, he's hitting .333.

Crowding the plate during his next time up, he's hit by a pitch. Like a walk, this does not count as an at-bat—but does count as a plate appearance—and therefore does not affect his average.

No outs, bases loaded for his third at-bat. He hits a dribbler back to the mound and reaches first base because the pitcher throws home to nail the lead runner. This is not a hit; it's a fielder's choice, and his 2-for-7 performance puts him at .286.

He starts the season's third game by lining out to the third baseman. He's now 2-for-8, batting .250.

Several innings later, with a man on third and one out, he hits a deep fly ball that allows the runner to tag up and score. Whether or not he meant to fly out for the good of the team, he gets credit for a sacrifice fly, and his average remains the same.

With two strikes in his following at-bat, he swings and misses at a slider in the dirt but makes it safely to first base when the ball gets past the catcher and scoots to the backstop.

This still counts as a strikeout. Now 2-for-9, his average dips to .222.

In his 10th at-bat of the season, he hits a routine foul pop-up, and the first baseman drops it. On the next pitch, he slugs a homer. Although the error prolonged his at-bat, he gets credit for a hit. At 3-for-10, he's batting .300. Phew!

Over the course of a 500-at-bat season, every hit is worth two points. If a batter were to squeak out one extra hit every two weeks—even a bunt down the third-base line or a broken-bat flare that dunks in front of the right fielder—he would raise his average by 24 points. Think about the difference between batting .277 and .301.

THE "ME! ME! ME!" OF BATTING AVERAGE

In today's game, where incentive-laden contracts rule, many guys selfishly play for their personal statistics at the expense of helping their team. Even in a close game, some players won't intentionally ground out to the right side to advance a runner to third because it would lower their batting average.

In the 1980s, Wade Boggs chose to sit out the final games of several seasons because his average was far enough ahead of other players that he was guaranteed to lead the league if it didn't drop.

Ted Williams, on the other hand, entered the last day of the 1941 season batting .3996 and was encouraged to take the day off so his average would round up to an even .400. He said no way, played both games of the *doubleheader*, went 6-for-8, and finished the season at .406—the last time anyone has batted over .400.

BATTING AVERAGE REFERENCE GUIDE

If a hitter is 3-for-11, is that any good? Quick! What's his average? It's easy to calculate if you know that 1-for-11 = .091. All you have to do is triple it, and you'll see that he's doing all right at .273. Here's a batting average reference guide:

1-for-1	1.000 →	1-for-11	.091
1-for-2	.500	1-for-12	.083
1-for-3	.333	1-for-13	.077
1-for-4	.250	1-for-14	.071
1-for-5	.200	1-for-15	.067
1-for-6	.167	1-for-16	.063
1-for-7	.143	1-for-17	.059
1-for-8	.125	1-for-18	.056
1-for-9	.111	1-for-19	.053
1-for-10	.100	1-for-20	.050

EARNED RUN AVERAGE

Earned run average measures the number of *earned runs* a pitcher allows every nine innings. To calculate it, multiply his earned runs by nine and then divide by the number of innings he's pitched. The formula: $(ER \times 9) \div IP$.

Why do stats specify that a run is earned? Suppose a batter reaches base on an error and the next guy up crushes a two-run homer. Is it fair to say that the pitcher allowed two runs? Yes. Were they both his fault? No. That's why runs allowed fall into two categories: earned and unearned. In this case, only one of the runs is earned—the home run—but had the error occurred with two outs, both runs would be unearned because the inning should have already ended.

Here are three other rules that determine whether a run is earned or unearned:

- If a passed ball allows an extra run, it's unearned.

- If a wild pitch allows an extra run, it's earned because it's the pitcher's fault.

- If the inning is prolonged by an error with two outs, all subsequent runs are unearned *unless* a relief pitcher enters the game. The reliever does not get the benefit of the assumed third out; all batters he faces are his responsibility, but his ERA will not suffer if he allows *inherited runners* to score. Those get charged to the pitcher who allowed them to reach base.

Sometimes you won't instantly know if a run is earned or unearned because it depends on what happens after. If a runner scores from third on a passed ball, and the next batter pokes a single through the infield, the run is earned because it would have scored anyway. But if the next batter flies out to end the inning, the run is unearned because it wouldn't have scored if not for the catcher's miscue.

EARNED RUN AVERAGE REFERENCE GUIDE

If a pitcher allows five runs in six-*plus* innings, what's his ERA? Use the following chart to figure it out quickly. Simply multiply 1.50 by 5 and you'll see that it's 7.50. (Keep in mind that "0.1 IP" means one-third of an inning pitched and "0.2 IP" means two-thirds.)

1 ER in 0.1 IP = 27.00	1 ER in 3.1 IP = 2.70	1 ER in 6.1 IP = 1.42
1 ER in 0.2 IP = 13.50	1 ER in 3.2 IP = 2.45	1 ER in 6.2 IP = 1.35
1 ER in 1.0 IP = 9.00	1 ER in 4.0 IP = 2.25	1 ER in 7.0 IP = 1.29
1 ER in 1.1 IP = 6.75	1 ER in 4.1 IP = 2.08	1 ER in 7.1 IP = 1.23
1 ER in 1.2 IP = 5.40	1 ER in 4.2 IP = 1.93	1 ER in 7.2 IP = 1.17
1 ER in 2.0 IP = 4.50	1 ER in 5.0 IP = 1.80	1 ER in 8.0 IP = 1.13
1 ER in 2.1 IP = 3.86	1 ER in 5.1 IP = 1.69	1 ER in 8.1 IP = 1.08
1 ER in 2.2 IP = 3.38	1 ER in 5.2 IP = 1.59	1 ER in 8.2 IP = 1.04
1 ER in 3.0 IP = 3.00 →	1 ER in 6.0 IP = 1.50	1 ER in 9.0 IP = 1.00

YOU STINK . . . I THINK

When a pitcher starts or enters the game, your television gets invaded by his statistics: games pitched, won-lost record, saves, earned run average, innings pitched, hits allowed, walks, and strikeouts. How can you tell if he's any good when there's so much to consider? Let's analyze the 2006 season totals of two pitchers, beginning with a starter named John Smoltz who's headed for the Hall of Fame:

YOUR TV SAYS:		THINGS TO CONSIDER:
G	35	Perfect for a starter in a five-man rotation, he made all of his starts.
W-L	16-9	A .640 winning percentage is superb; first-place teams end up around .600.
S	0	Of course he doesn't have any saves. His job is to start, not finish games.
ERA	3.49	Not bad. Anything under 4.00 is respectable, but under 3.00 is fantastic.
IP	232	Anything over 200 is solid. He averaged almost 6.2 innings per start.
H	221	The pitcher's doing something right when he allows less than one hit per inning.
BB	55	2.1 walks per nine innings is excellent. Also look at his SO/BB ratio.
SO	211	In general, a 2-to-1 SO/BB ratio is good. His 3.8-to-1 ratio is terrific. Few pitchers average more than one strikeout per inning. Smoltz is pretty close.

Now, here are the stats of Ryan Dempster, a reliever whom many people—especially in Chicago—would like to forget:

YOUR TV SAYS:		THINGS TO CONSIDER:
G	74	Yeah, it's a lot of games, but so what, he's a reliever.
W-L	1-9	Two words: Minor Leagues.
S	24	This is a decent total, but he also blew nine saves. Yikes.
ERA	4.80	Lousy, but much better than his nightmarish 6.54 ERA in 2003.
IP	75	Never judge relievers by their innings pitched (although 100 is a lot).
H	77	Not a disaster, but allowing more than a hit per inning is nothing to brag about.
BB	36	Almost one walk every two innings . . . not good.
SO	67	A 1.9-to-1 SO/BB ratio? Snore.

R-O-L-A-I-D-S SPELLS RELIEF

In 1960 *The Sporting News* created the *Fireman* of the Year Award for the best relief pitcher in each league. In 1976 an antacid manufacturer called Rolaids established the more popular Rolaids Relief Man Award. Still recognized today, the Rolaids award is given to the pitcher who scores highest under the following system:

ADD:	SUBTRACT:
4 points for a *tough save*	2 points for a blown save
3 points for every other save	2 points for a loss
2 points for a win	

In 2003 Eric Gagne set the record for most points with 165. The lowest score for a winner of the award (with the exception of Bruce Sutter's 51 points during the strike-shortened 1981 season) is 59 points by Hall of Famer Rollie Fingers, set in 1980 when the scoring system wasn't as generous.

But wait. What the heck is a save? It's a statistic awarded to a relief pitcher who does all three of these things:

- He finishes a game that his team wins.

- He's not the winning pitcher.

- He meets one of the following three conditions:

  1. He enters the game with his team leading by three runs or less and pitches at least one inning.

  2. He enters the game with the potential tying run on base, at bat, or on deck. (In other words, he enters the game with a five-run lead and the bases loaded or a four-run lead with two guys on base, etc.)

  3. He pitches at least three innings.

THE OFFICIAL SCORER

Little Leaguers lead lives of defensive ignorance, making excuses for themselves by saying, "It's not an error if the ball doesn't touch your glove." True, a batted ball that whizzes beyond an outstretched glove is not an error, but does it make sense to give the batter credit for a hit if his routine pop-up lands untouched at a fielder's feet? No.

In the majors, a play that cannot be handled with "ordinary effort" is supposed to be ruled a base hit. Who decides what qualifies as ordinary? The official scorer. Chosen by the home team and approved by the league, he gets paid $130 per game to keep track of the action and determine how it breaks down into statistical categories.

For an error to be charged, a physical misplay must result in at least one of the following:

- The batter's plate appearance is prolonged. (If the fielding team drops a foul pop-up, the batter gets to stay at the plate longer than he should have.)
- The batter reaches base when he should have been out. (An outfielder boots an easy fly ball.)
- The runner advances an extra base when he should have been held where he was. (The batter hits a ground ball single up the middle, the center fielder's return throw to the infield gets loose, and the batter makes it to second base. This is scored as a hit *and* an error.)
- The runner's life is prolonged. (He gets caught in a rundown, and the throw beats him back to the base, but it's dropped, and he's safe.)

Here are some rules that guide the scorer in assigning blame:

- If a ground ball takes a bad hop, it's a hit.
- If an outfielder drops a fly ball because he was looking into the sun, it can be a hit or an error.
- If a fielder handles a play slowly (failing to charge the ball, for example) but commits no physical blunder, it's a hit.
- Mental errors (such as forgetting to cover a base) are not recorded, but the player still gets booed by the fans and yelled at by his manager.

- A double play cannot be assumed.[2] This means that if the first baseman drops a perfect throw after the middle infielders have already recorded one out on the play, he might not be charged with an error.

- If a throw sails high or wide or bounces before reaching its target, the error goes to the player who threw it. (The same rule applies when deciding whether to charge the pitcher with a wild pitch or the catcher with a passed ball.)

- When a routine fly ball or pop-up lands between several uncommunicative players, it can be a hit or it can be an error for the fielder who was standing closest to it.

Here are some rules that help the scorer calculate stats:

- When the pitcher falls behind in the count and then decides to intentionally walk the batter, it counts as an intentional walk.

- When a runner gets picked off, it counts as a caught stealing if he first moved toward the next base.

- When one runner gets thrown out on a double steal, the other runner does not get credit for a stolen base.

- When a run scores on a double play or an error, the batter does not get a *run batted in*. When he walks or gets hit by a pitch with the bases loaded, he does.

- When the ball deflects off a fielder and bounces to his teammate who records an out, the first fielder gets an assist. If an outfielder *hits the cutoff man,* and the cutoff man throws out a runner, both guys get assists.

- When a pinch-hitter is announced but gets replaced before stepping to the plate, he is still considered to have appeared in the game. (This happens more than you

[2]Author's opinion: this is a stupid rule.

might think, as managers jockey for the righty-lefty advantage by using various pitchers and pinch-hitters.)

- When the manager gets ejected, he still gets the win or loss.

Unfortunately, politics often invades the official scorer's job. Not only do players and coaches occasionally call him between innings or after the game (and, in extreme cases, make obscene gestures at him from the field) to express their displeasure, but he's almost forced to give certain players the benefit of the doubt. If the home team's pitcher takes a *no-hitter* late into the game and the scorer needs to make a borderline hit-versus-error decision, he undoubtedly feels pressured to do what's necessary to keep the pitcher's gem intact. Or if a batter needs a hit in his final at-bat to extend his *hitting streak,* any close ruling pretty much has to go in his favor. But don't worry—if the scorer feels guilty about making a hometown call, he has 24 hours to reverse his decision.

HOW TO KEEP SCORE

The best way to keep your head in the game is to write down everything that happens by using a specific set of symbols and abbreviations. This is called *keeping score.* You don't have to do it. In fact, most fans don't. They either don't know how or don't care—for any number of sensible reasons. So feel free to skip this section.

Or keep reading. And consider that everyone who keeps score uses a slightly different method. If you'd like to give it a shot, play around with it until you find a system that makes the most sense. But keep in mind that some symbols are universal, such as the numbers that represent defensive positions and some of the abbreviations for the action:

POSITIONS	ABBREVIATIONS	
1 = Pitcher	Single = 1B	Sacrifice fly = SF
2 = Catcher	Double = 2B	Hit by pitch = HP
3 = First baseman	Triple = 3B	Fielder's choice = FC
4 = Second baseman	Home run = HR	Line drive out = L
5 = Third baseman	Walk = BB	Flyout = F
6 = Shortstop	Intentional walk = IBB	Pop out = P
7 = Left fielder	Stolen base = SB	Error = E
8 = Center fielder	Caught stealing = CS	Double play = DP
9 = Right fielder	Swinging strikeout = K	Triple play = TP
	Called strikeout = Ʞ	Balk = BK
	Wild pitch = WP	Unassisted = U
	Passed ball = PB	Defensive indifference = DI
	Sacrifice bunt = SAC	Picked off = PK

So, for example, if the batter grounds out to the pitcher, write "1–3" to indicate that he was thrown out at first base. If he grounds out to the first baseman, who jogs to the bag and makes the play by himself, write "3U." If he hits a single, draw a tiny base path from home to first and write "1B" next to it. If he advances to second on a wild pitch, draw the base path from first to second and write "WP." If the catcher fields a bunt and throws him out at third, draw half the baseline from second to third with a slash and write "2–5." When a runner scores, draw the entire diamond and color it in.

After each inning, write the number of hits, runs, errors, and runners left on base. After the game, calculate the totals. Using the method of your choice, keep track of *RBIs* (some people like to write little ticks next to the player's name) and all the pitchers' stats in the boxes provided. If there's anything else you'd like to remember, go for it.

If the team *bats around,* cross out and rewrite the inning numbers at the top of the columns to give yourself more room. If there's a substitution, write the new player's name below that of the guy he replaces, along with the number of the inning in which he enters the game.

Here's a sample score sheet:

FIRST INNING:

Hernandez	Lines out to the right fielder.
Gonzalez	Gets hit by a pitch.
Rodriguez	Grounds to the third baseman, who throws to second to force out the lead runner.
Ramirez	Takes a called third strike.

SECOND INNING:

Fernandez	Singles.
Martinez	Hits a sacrifice bunt to the first baseman. The second baseman takes the throw at first base.
Ordonez	Hits a *squibber* in front of home plate. The catcher grabs it and tags him out.
Ibanez	Gets intentionally walked.
Benitez	Hits a three-run homer.
Hernandez	Reaches base on an error by the shortstop, steals second, and goes to third on a balk.
Tavarez	Pinch-hits for Gonzalez and flies out to the left fielder.

LINE UP	POS	1	2	3
Hernandez	SS	L9	BK SB E-6	
Gonzalez	2B	5-4 HP	F7	
Tavarez PH(2)				
Rodriguez	RF	FC		
Ramirez	LF	K		
Fernandez	C		1B	
Martinez	3B		SAC 3-4	
Ordonez	1B		2u	
Ibanez	CF		1BB	
Benitez	P		HR	
TOTALS — RUNS		0	3	
H E LOB	0 0	0 1 2	1 1	

HOW TO READ A BOX SCORE

A box score is a condensed statistical recap of a game's action. You can find box scores online and in newspapers. Or you can avoid them (and this section) altogether. But if you want to learn how to read them—how a strange jumble of names and numbers and abbreviations can deliver the highlights and reveal clues that fill in the gaps—check out this box score and the notes that go with it:

PART ONE

Stats for this game. "BI" means "RBI."

Total batting average for the season.

Apparently, he was used only as a late-inning defensive replacement.

Entered the game as a pinch-hitter.

Started the game in left field, finished the game at first base.

Entered the game as a pinch-runner.

He's probably 1-for-2 this year, not 46-for-92.

No batting average because he hasn't had any at-bats all season.

This game, the Expos went 16-for-39. That's a batting average of .410. Wow!

EXPOS 12, PADRES 9

San Diego	AB	R	H	BI	BB	SO	Avg.
Victorino lf	4	0	0	0	0	0	.205
f-Lockhart ph	1	1	1	0	0	0	.243
Orosco p	0	0	0	0	0	0	—
Merloni 3b	0	0	0	0	0	0	.267
Loretta 2b	3	1	0	0	1	1	.273
RVazquez ss	5	0	1	2	0	2	.274
Klesko 1b	3	3	1	2	2	0	.271
Kotsay cf	5	2	2	0	0	0	.270
Burroughs 3b	4	0	2	1	1	1	.216
JSWright p	0	0	0	0	0	0	.500
Nady rf	5	1	2	2	0	1	.269
WGonzalez c	5	0	1	2	0	0	.204
Condrey p	2	0	0	0	0	2	.250
MMatthews p	0	0	0	0	0	0	.000
Villafuerte p	0	0	0	0	0	0	—
a-Buchanan ph	1	0	0	0	0	0	.267
Hackman p	0	0	0	0	0	0	.000
Herges p	0	0	0	0	0	0	—
e-Hansen ph	1	1	1	0	0	0	.250
White lf	0	0	0	0	0	0	.239
Totals	**39**	**9**	**11**	**9**	**4**	**7**	

Montreal	AB	R	H	BI	BB	SO	Avg.
EnChavez cf	4	1	1	0	2	0	.283
OCabrera ss	6	3	4	2	0	1	.281
Vidro 2b	6	2	3	1	0	0	.342
VGuerrero rf	4	3	2	3	2	0	.280
Wilkerson lf-1b	2	2	2	4	2	0	.309
WCordero 1b	3	0	2	1	1	0	.264
1-Carroll pr	0	1	0	0	0	0	.267
Ayala p	0	0	0	0	0	0	—
d-Macias ph	1	0	0	0	0	0	.212
Biddle p	0	0	0	0	0	0	—
Tatis 3b	5	0	2	0	0	0	.252
Schneider c	4	0	0	0	1	1	.208
Day p	2	0	0	0	0	1	.000
Eischen p	0	0	0	0	0	0	—
Tucker p	0	0	0	0	0	0	.000
b-HMateo ph	1	0	0	0	0	0	.409
ScStewart p	0	0	0	0	0	0	.000
c-Calloway ph-lf	1	0	0	1	0	0	.244
Totals	**39**	**12**	**16**	**12**	**8**	**4**	

San Diego	200	203	002	0—	9	11	2	
Montreal	021	041	100	3—12	16	1		

Entered the game as a pinch-runner.

The Padres scored twice in the top of the 1st inning. The Expos scored twice in the bottom of the 2nd and once in the 3rd.

Totals for the game: 9 runs, 11 hits, 2 errors.

PART TWO

There was one out when Guerrero hit his three-run, walk-off homer in the bottom of the 10th.

Tells you what the pinch-hitters and pinch-runner did.

Committed his third error of the season.

Hit two doubles, giving him 16 this season.

The Expos left nine men on base.

Hit his ninth home run of the season, and this one was against Day.

Same as "SAC."

Grounded into two double plays.

Each of these guys made the third out of an inning with a runner on 2nd or 3rd base.

The Padres turned two 4-6-3 double plays.

One out when winning run scored. a-flied out for Villafuerte in the 6th. b-grounded out for Tucker in the 6th. c-hit a sacrifice fly for Stewart in the 7th. d-grounded out for Ayala in the 8th. e-singled for Herges in the 9th. f-singled for Victorino in the 9th. 1-ran for Cordero in the 7th. **E**—Burroughs (3), WGonzalez (1), Wilkerson (2). **LOB**—San Diego 5, Montreal 9. **2B**—RVazquez (7), Burroughs (7), OCabrera 2 (8), Vidro 2 (16), Wilkerson (10), WCordero 2 (3). **HR**—VGuerrero (6), off JSWright; OCabrera (5), off Condrey; Wilkerson (5), off Condrey; Klesko (9), off Day. **RBIs**—RVazquez 2 (15), Klesko 2 (26), Burroughs (11), Nady 2 (9), WGonzalez 2 (10), OCabrera 2 (20), Vidro (14), VGuerrero 3 (20), Wilkerson 4 (22), WCordero (10), Calloway (6). **SB**—EnChavez (4). **CS**—VGuerrero (2). **S**—Loretta. **SF**—Calloway. **GIDP**—WGonzalez, Schneider 2. **Runners left in scoring position**—San Diego 3 (Kotsay, WGonzalez, Condrey); Montreal 3 (OCabrera, WCordero, Day). **Runners moved up**—VGuerrero, Tatis. **DP**—San Diego 2 (Loretta, RVazquez and Klesko), (Loretta, RVazquez and Klesko); Montreal 1 (Day, OCabrera, Vidro and WCordero).

PART THREE

Stats for this game.

Total earned run average for the season.

Lost the game. His season record is now zero wins and one loss.

Needed to throw 27 pitches just to get through one inning.

Blew a save for the first time this year by allowing the Padres to tie the game with two runs in the top of the 9th, but he stayed in the game, pitched a scoreless 10th, and got the win when his team scored in the bottom of the inning.

Allowed one run, but it was unearned.

And he allowed them both to reach base.

Entered the game with two runners on base and allowed them both to score.

San Diego	IP	H	R	ER	BB	SO	NP	ERA
Condrey	4⅓	7	6	6	2	2	70	8.36
MMatthews	0	1	1	0	0	0	3	4.29
Villafuerte	⅔	2	0	0	0	0	9	5.06
Hackman	1	2	1	1	2	0	27	3.50
Herges	2	2	1	1	3	0	54	1.10
Orosco L, 0-1	1	1	2	2	1	2	22	5.56
JSWright	⅓	1	1	1	0	7	5.29
Montreal	IP	H	R	ER	BB	SO	NP	ERA
Day	5	5	6	6	4	3	84	2.89
Eischen BS, 2	⅓	2	1	0	0	0	15	0.69
Tucker	⅔	0	0	0	0	0	7	3.31
ScStewart H, 6	1	0	0	0	0	2	11	1.13
Ayala H, 4	1	1	0	0	0	0	18	4.32
Biddle W, 3-1 BS, 12	3	2	2	0	2	33	4.42

MMatthews pitched to 1 batter in the 5th, Orosco pitched to 2 batters in the 10th, Day pitched to 2 batters in the 6th.
Inherited runners-scored—JSWright 2-1, MMatthews 2-2, Villafuerte 1-1, Eischen 2-2, Tucker 1-0. **IBB**—off Herges (Schneider) 1, off Condrey (VGuerrero) 1. **HBP**—by Condrey (Wilkerson). **WP**—MMatthews. **Umpires**—Home, Sam Holbrook; First, Paul Schrieber; Second, Angel Hernandez; Third, Randy Marsh. **T**—3:35. **A**—5,111 (46,338).

Threw a wild pitch—one of only three pitches he threw all game.

Attendance

Seating capacity

The game lasted three hours and 35 minutes.

LEADING THE LEAGUE

In 1990 Willie McGee collected 199 hits in 614 at-bats for a .324 batting average. Even though Eddie Murray finished at .330, Dave Magadan at .328, and Lenny Dykstra at .325, McGee won the NL batting title with his .335 average. How was this possible? McGee had gone 168-for-501 (.335) when the Cardinals traded him to the A's, where he finished 31-for-113 (.274) in his final 29 games. Because players' stats reset when they switch leagues, McGee's NL average froze when he headed to the West Coast. Did he deserve the *batting crown* even though he didn't play the complete season in the NL?

Yes.

But what if someone goes 5-for-8 in the season's first two games before getting traded or injured—would he lead the league with a .625 average? How about if a pitcher retires his first hitter of the year and then quits—would his 0.00 ERA put him above all others?

No and no.

To qualify as the league leader for an offensive percentage (AVG, SLG, OBP, OPS, HR/AB, etc.), a batter must average at least 3.1 plate appearances per game that his team plays. That's 502 plate appearances in a 162-game season. McGee had just 501 at-bats, but his 38 walks counted as plate appearances, as did his two sac flies and lone hit by a pitch. Meanwhile, a pitcher must average at least one inning for each of his team's games to qualify for stats like ERA, WHIP, and K/9.

When a player is traded to a team within his league, his stats do not reset—except on the back of his baseball card, where each team gets its own line. It always looks ugly.

INCREDIBLE FEATS

One great thing about watching baseball is the chance to see something historic at any moment. A future Hall of Famer might reach a statistical milestone, or a *journeyman* could dazzle you with a single play. You never know, so pay attention and look for one of these incredible feats.

A PERFECT GAME This is the pitcher's ultimate accomplishment. It's a complete game in which he faces the minimum number of batters (27 in nine innings) and does not allow any of them to reach base. A perfect game is so rare that it happens just once or twice per decade, and only one pitcher has achieved perfection in the postseason: Don Larsen in Game 5 of the 1956 World Series. Several pitchers have taken perfect games into extra innings before allowing a base runner; in 1959 Harvey Haddix lasted until the 13th. In 1917 Babe Ruth (who began his career as a successful pitcher) walked the first batter of a game and got ejected for arguing and slugging the umpire. Ernie Shore replaced Ruth, nabbed the base runner in his attempt to steal, and retired the final 26 batters. Is that a perfect game? Maybe, but with an asterisk.

A NO-HITTER When the pitcher throws a complete game without allowing a hit, it's called a no-hitter. It differs from a perfect game because batters can draw walks, get hit by pitches, reach base on errors, lay down sacrifice bunts, steal bases, and even score.[3] Still, there are usually just one or two no-hitters each

[3] In 1990 Yankees pitcher Andy Hawkins tossed a no-hitter against the White Sox and lost, 4–0, after things fell apart in the eighth inning. Third baseman Mike Blowers booted Sammy Sosa's grounder, and Hawkins walked two batters to load the bases. Outfielders Jim Leyritz and Jesse Barfield then dropped back-to-back fly balls to allow all four runs to score. This game remains the biggest margin of defeat for any pitcher who's thrown a no-hitter.

season. Nolan Ryan holds the career record with seven, and Sandy Koufax threw four. In 1938 Johnny Vander Meer became the only guy to hurl no-hitters in back-to-back starts. In 2003 after Astros starter Roy Oswalt went down with an injury in the second inning—a strained groin, if you really want to know—a record six pitchers combined to no-hit the Yankees.

THE CYCLE Slightly more common than a no-hitter is a batter hitting a single, double, triple, and home run in one game (though not necessarily in that order). It's called *hitting for the cycle,* and two players have accomplished the feat three times: Bob Meusel and Babe Herman.[4] In 1931 Herman became the only player to do it twice in one season.

FOUR HOME RUNS IN ONE GAME In 1999 a college player named Marshall McDougall hit six home runs in one game, two more than the major league record. Of the 15 major leaguers with four-homer games, six needed just four at-bats. More than 20 players have hit five *taters* in back-to-back games, but only Stan Musial (1954) and Nate Colbert (1972) did it in a doubleheader.

AN INSIDE-THE-PARK HOME RUN This kind of home run was common in the old days because ballparks were bigger and it took a while for gappers to stop rolling. Nowadays, we're lucky to see more than one or two per season, and when we do, it's always the result of a misplay that wasn't bad enough to be ruled an error. (An outfielder might run in and dive for a sinking line drive that scoots under his glove and rolls all the way back to the wall.) Sam Crawford, who began his career in 1899, holds both the single-season record (12) and

[4] Babe Herman is not Babe Ruth. These are two different guys. People sometimes get confused because Ruth's middle name was Herman.

the career record (51) for inside-the-parkers. The last player to hit two in one game was Greg Gagne in 1986. Hank Aaron had just one in his entire career.

AN UNASSISTED TRIPLE PLAY There are usually one or two triple plays each year, but only a dozen have ever been made without a throw. They're called unassisted triple plays, and here's how it happens: With no outs, runners on first and second take off for second and third. A middle infielder darts toward second to receive the throw from the catcher, but the batter hits a line drive up the middle right to him. He catches the ball (one out), steps on second to force out the runner who broke toward third (two outs), and tags the other runner barreling toward him from first (three outs). Two first basemen have turned unassisted triple plays: George Burns in 1923 and Johnny Neun in 1927. The rest have been made by middle infielders.

THE 30/30 CLUB This recognizes players who hit 30 or more home runs and steal 30 or more bases in one season, an impressive accomplishment because few guys possess both the speed and the power to put up such numbers. More than two dozen players have done it, starting with Ken Williams in 1922. Bobby Bonds and his son Barry share the record with five 30/30 seasons each. In 1988 Jose Canseco became the first to reach 40/40, and three other players have joined him: Barry Bonds in 1996, Alex Rodriguez in 1998, and Alfonso Soriano in 2006. Only six men have reached 300/300 for their careers: Willie Mays, Bobby Bonds, Andre Dawson, Reggie Sanders, Steve Finley, and Barry Bonds, who made it to 500/500.

THE TRIPLE CROWN (hitting) More of an honor than an actual award, this goes to a batter who, in one season, leads (or ties) the league in home runs, *runs batted in,* and batting average. So few players hit for both power and average that no one has won this award since Carl Yastrzemski in 1967. (The last National League winner was Joe "Ducky" Medwick in 1937.) Only Rogers Hornsby and Ted Williams have won it twice.

THE TRIPLE CROWN (pitching) This goes to a pitcher who leads (or ties) the league in wins, strikeouts, and earned run average. Four players have won the award in consecutive seasons: Grover "Pete" Alexander (1915–16), Lefty Grove (1930–31), Sandy Koufax (1965–66), and Roger Clemens (1997–98). Alexander, Koufax, and Walter Johnson are the only guys to win it three times overall.

FOUR STRIKEOUTS IN ONE INNING When the catcher drops the third strike (or if the ball bounces before it reaches him), the batter can run to first base unless there's already a runner there with less than two outs. If he makes it safely by beating the catcher's throw, the pitcher still gets credit for a strikeout, and the official scorer assigns a wild pitch or passed ball. More than forty pitchers have struck out four batters in one inning. No one's accomplished the feat more than once except Chuck Finley, who did it three times: twice in 1999 and once in 2000.

A HITTING STREAK This measures the number of consecutive games in which a batter gets at least one hit. Here are two important rules:

- He can take a day off (or a month off) and keep his streak intact because it's all about *his* games, not the team's.

- If he plays a game in which his only plate appearances result in walks, sacrifice bunts, hit by pitches, and defensive interference, his streak stays alive because of his lack of opportunity to swing the bat.

Fans love hitting streaks, and the whole country went nuts in 1941 when Joe DiMaggio batted safely in 56 straight games, breaking the old record of 44 games, which had been set in 1897 by "Wee" Willie Keeler.[5] Only four other players have accomplished 40-game streaks: Pete Rose (44 in 1978), Bill Dahlen (42 in 1894), George Sisler (41 in 1922), and Ty Cobb (40 in 1911). Benito Santiago holds the rookie record of 34 games in 1987, and by the way, DiMaggio had a 61-game streak in the minors.

A SCORELESS INNINGS STREAK In 1913 Walter Johnson set a record by pitching 55.2 consecutive scoreless innings. Fifty-five years later, Don Drysdale passed him with a 58.2-inning streak. Everyone thought the new record was unbreakable, but Orel Hershiser proved otherwise in 1988 when he pitched 10 shutout innings in his last game of the season to eclipse Drysdale's mark by one third of an inning. In the first inning of his first game the following season, Hershiser allowed a run, and his streak died at 59.

A CONSECUTIVE GAME STREAK Seven men have played in over 1,000 consecutive games. Lou Gehrig, nicknamed "The Iron Horse," held the record at 2,130 for more than half a century until Cal Ripken Jr. stunned the baseball world by

---

[5]One of the smallest players in history at 5-foot-4, 140 pounds, Keeler famously explained the key to his success: "I keep my eyes clear and I hit 'em where they ain't." As a member of the Orioles in the 1890s, Keeler would swing down at the ball and bounce it high off the hard dirt around home plate. John McGraw, his teammate—and fellow Hall of Famer—did it too, and the hit became known as the "Baltimore Chop."

passing him in 1995 and extending his streak to 2,632. Why is this impressive? Because baseball, unlike other sports, has a merciless schedule with games almost every day; without time to rest, minor pains become nagging injuries. It's also easy to get hurt. A player might foul a ball off his foot and lose sensation in his toes, get hit by a 96-mph fastball and have a bruise the size of a cantaloupe, pull a muscle while trying to score from first base on a double, twist his ankle when his spikes stick in the dirt on a slide, and smack his chin on the ground while diving awkwardly for a ball—and that's all before the third inning.

CHAPTER 9
RANDOM STUFF TO KNOW

A slick way to outfigure a person is to get him figuring you figure he's figuring you're figuring he'll figure you aren't really figuring what you want him to figure you figure.

—Whitey Herzog, former manager

GRAB *THIS*

What's the deal with guys who grab and scratch their crotches on national television? Aren't their mothers ashamed?

Players could be more discreet about it by ducking into the *runways* or saving their fondling for commercial breaks, but we fans need to give them a break. They make certain adjustments to ease the discomfort from wearing big, awkward plastic protective cups in their underwear. (Of course, they'd feel even more discomfort if they got hit there without the protection.) Although the cup fits snugly into a special pouch, its foam-covered edges often rub and chafe the insides of the upper thighs. And that's before it inevitably slips slightly out of place.

Outfielders rarely get hit in the groin, so they can play cup-free. Infielders can't. They need to guard against the constant threat of bad hops. In particular, the catcher, with foul tips and 55-footers whizzing at him, needs the protection more than anyone.

"K"

If you think a strikeout is called a "K" because of Matt Kilroy, the first real strikeout pitcher, who *fanned* 513 batters in 1886[1] for the Baltimore Orioles of the American Association, you're wrong.

"K" was chosen by a British-born journalist named Henry Chadwick, who developed a scoring system in 1861. His simple explanation: "It was the prominent letter of the word 'strike,' as far as remembering the word was concerned."

Nowadays, fans sometimes bring homemade "K" signs to the ballpark and tape them to the walls or to the facades of upper seating levels as batters on the visiting team strike out. Some fans reverse the third "K" sign so people won't think they're Ku Klux Klan members—but remember that a backward "K" also indicates a called third strike.

UNWRITTEN RULES

Baseball has many unwritten rules involving respect: Don't stand in the batter's box and watch your *moon shot* sail over the wall. Don't trot too slowly around the bases. Don't act excited after striking out the hitter. Don't try to steal the catcher's signs. Don't hide in the dugout or bullpen if everyone else on

---

[1] Yeah, the mound was 10½ feet closer back then, but you have to give the guy some credit. He also pitched 66 complete games, and this was his rookie year.

the team runs onto the field for a brawl. Don't draw a line in the dirt to show the umpire that strike three was actually four inches off the plate. And so on.

A famous etiquette-related controversy occurred at San Diego's Qualcomm Stadium in 2001. Diamondbacks pitcher Curt Schilling was dominating the Padres—it took them four innings to hit the ball out of the infield—and when he was just five outs away from throwing the 15th perfect game in major league history, Padres catcher Ben Davis broke up the gem with a bunt base hit. Arizona was furious that he ruined the potentially historic performance without "earning" his way on base. After the game, Arizona manager Bob Brenly said, "Ben Davis is young and has a lot to learn. That was just uncalled for."

It's true that breaking up a no-hitter with a bunt is normally frowned upon, but this situation was different. Apparently, Brenly forgot that the Padres were trailing, 2–0, and that Davis brought the tying run to the plate by reaching base. He also forgot how important this game was: the two teams were tied for first place.

In another well-known etiquette squabble involving a member of the 2001 Padres, all-time stolen base leader Rickey Henderson swiped second when his team had a 12–5 lead in the seventh inning. Davey Lopes, the Brewers manager, was so angry at Henderson for stealing with his team already winning by seven runs that he stormed onto the field and threatened to have his pitchers *drill* him during his next at-bat. (Padres manager Bruce Botchy removed Henderson from the game, and the league later fined Lopes and suspended him for two games.)

Teams have historically avoided running up the score in the late innings of *laughers,* but we're now in an era of inflated offense. There's no such thing as too many *insurance runs* because no lead is safe. Apparently, Lopes forgot that on the previous day the Pirates were down to their final out with no one on base when they started a seven-run *rally* and beat the Astros, 9–8. One week later, the Indians tied the biggest comeback in major league history when they recovered from a 14–2 deficit in the seventh and defeated the Mariners, 15–14, in 11 innings.

Most fans, and even some players, believe that while it's ungentlemanly to humiliate anyone, the unwritten rules have gone too far. In the big leagues, the goal should be winning, not worrying about making the other guys feel bad.

CITIES AND NAMES

The Los Angeles Dodgers haven't always been the Los Angeles Dodgers. They were the Brooklyn Dodgers from 1932 to 1957 and the Brooklyn Robins for 18 years before that. Earlier still, when people didn't worry as much about being dorky, the team used names like Superbas, Bridegrooms, and Trolley Dodgers.

The Cubs used to be called the Orphans. The Astros were the Colt 45s. The Cardinals were the Perfectos. The Indians were the Naps. The White Sox were the White Stockings. The Reds were the Redlegs. The Pirates were the Alleghenys. The Yankees were the Highlanders. The Braves first played in Boston, then Milwaukee, and tried names like Bees, Rustlers, Doves, Beaneaters, and Red Caps. Both the Twins and Rangers played in Washington, D.C.—though not at the same time—as the Senators. The Athletics originally played in Philadelphia and later in Kansas City. The Brewers spent one season in Seattle and called themselves the Pilots.

It's amusing to look back at who was called what and played where, but it was no joke to the fans who watched helplessly as their beloved teams moved away. Many New Yorkers are still heartbroken that the Dodgers took off for the West Coast, and if that weren't enough, the New York Giants (once called the New York Gothams), who'd belonged to the city since 1883, moved to San Francisco the same year.

These days, teams rarely move because MLB forces new owners to sign lengthy leases for their ballparks. Unfortunately, no one can stop an owner from changing his team's name to make it look like he's moved. In a marketing ploy designed to entice sponsors in two different cities before the 2005 season, the Anaheim Angels became the Los Angeles Angels of Anaheim. Ouch.

THE ROOKIE OF THE YEAR AWARD

The first Rookie of the Year Award was especially well deserved. It went to Brooklyn Dodgers first baseman Jackie Robinson, who in 1947 not only put up great numbers and led his team to the first televised World Series but showed extraordinary courage in becoming the first African-American major leaguer in the modern era.[2] Two years later, Roy Sievers, an outfielder on the St. Louis Browns, became the first American League recipient when the award started going to one player in each league.

Members of the BBWAA used to make their selections by simply picking one player each. But after a tie in 1979 between Twins third baseman John Castino and Blue Jays shortstop Alfredo Griffin, the voting process became more

[2]Fleet Walker is credited as being the first of all time. In 1884 the twenty-seven-year-old catcher appeared in forty-two games with the Toledo Blue-Stockings of the American Association.

complex. Each writer began making a first choice worth five points, a second choice worth three, and a third choice worth one. Overall, there have been 15 unanimous selections, and the award was officially named after Robinson in 1987.

But wait. If a guy plays two games all year, does that count as his rookie season? No. He'll still be eligible for the award the following season as long as he doesn't fall into any of these categories:

- Hitters with 130 or more career at-bats

- Pitchers with 50 or more career innings pitched

- Anyone who's spent 45 or more days on a major league roster

THE MOST VALUABLE PLAYER AWARD

There have been three different Most Valuable Player Awards since 1911, but the current one is the only one that counts. It started in 1931 when the BBWAA selected the first two recipients—pitcher Lefty Grove of the AL's Philadelphia Athletics and second baseman Frankie Frisch of the NL's St. Louis Cardinals—and people are still arguing over what makes a guy valuable. Does he deserves the MVP if he leads the league in every category but plays on a last-place team? And what about pitchers? Should they be considered? They do have their own award, after all.

Some notable MVP winners include Frank Robinson, the only player to claim the honor in both leagues; Fred Lynn and Ichiro Suzuki, the only two rookies; and Barry Bonds, the only man to win it four consecutive seasons and seven times overall (no one else has won more than three).

THE ALL-STAR GAME

The All-Star Game, an exhibition between the best players in each league, takes place roughly halfway through the season, each year at a different ballpark. Fans select the starting position players by voting online and at games. The previous season's World Series managers get to call the shots and pick their coaches, pitchers, and reserve position players. Every team in the league must be represented by at least one player, a controversial rule because the limited number of roster spots forces each manager to snub several deserving players for weaker ones who must be chosen.

The first All-Star Game was played at Chicago's Comiskey Park in 1933. At the following season's contest, New York Giants left-hander Carl Hubbell made history by striking out five consecutive future Hall of Famers: Babe Ruth, Lou Gehrig, Jimmie Foxx, Al Simmons, and Joe Cronin. Throughout the years, the *Midsummer Classic* has remained a fan favorite, and a new rule in 2003 made the game even more exciting: the league that wins gets home-field advantage in the following World Series.

THE HALL OF FAME

In 1936 the National Baseball Hall of Fame welcomed its first five members—Ty Cobb, Babe Ruth, Honus Wagner, Christy Mathewson, and Walter Johnson—and the famous museum opened three years later. Located in Cooperstown, New York, where Civil War general Abner Doubleday was once believed to have invented the sport in

1839,[3] the Hall of Fame now has more than 275 members and attracts 350,000 visitors every year, many of whom show up for Hall of Fame Weekend, when the newly elected members are officially inducted.

In order to have a shot at the Hall, a player needs at least 10 years of major league experience. Then, after five years in retirement, he gets added to the ballot. Every member of the BBWAA gets to vote for 10 players each year. Any player who receives at least 75 percent of the vote is in; any player who receives less than 5 percent of the vote gets kicked off the ballot. A player also gets booted off the ballot after 15 years, although he can still be voted in by the *Veterans Committee,* which consists of Hall-of-Fame players, managers, writers, and broadcasters. (There are also some umpires and baseball executives in the Hall.) Many people—especially BBWAA members—wonder why the 15-year rule exists in the first place.

Although the museum displays game-used artifacts and equipment (like the glove of a pitcher who tossed a no-hitter), the players who used them are not necessarily Hall of Famers, because the voting is based on entire careers rather than single-game and single-season accomplishments. According to the Hall of Fame, the considerations include "the player's record, playing ability, integrity, sportsmanship, character, and contributions to the team(s) on which the player played."

Everyone accepts that certain numbers—500 home runs, 3,000 hits, and 300 wins—are guaranteed tickets to

[3]Alexander Cartwright, who in 1845 invented the modern baseball field and published the first set of widely used baseball rules, is now credited with having invented the sport. One year later, his team, the Knickerbockers, played—and lost—the first recorded game against the New York Baseball Club at the Elysian Fields in Hoboken, New Jersey.

Cooperstown, but some people feel that statistics carry too much weight. Why, for example, isn't Bert Blyleven enshrined? Apparently, his 3,701 strikeouts (fifth all time) and 287 victories were not enough of a contribution to his teams. But is 287 that far away from the magical 300? What about Tommy John? He won 288 games. How come he's not in the Hall? Perhaps it's because he pitched for 26 seasons and achieved his numbers more through longevity than extraordinary skill. Meanwhile, Sandy Koufax, with only 165 career wins, was an obvious choice for induction because he dominated the sport during his prime.

UNIFORM NUMBERS

At the turn of the 20th century, several teams briefly experimented with putting numbers on their players' uniforms. It didn't go over too well. The players complained that the numbers made them look like convicts, but still, the concept stayed alive, and on April 16, 1929, the Indians became the first team to wear them permanently—for home games only. The Yankees, who sported the look two days later, were the first to do so both at home and on the road. In 1934 the Giants became the last team to adopt the trend.

Early numbers were assigned based on the batting order; Babe Ruth hit third for the Yankees and took number 3, while Lou Gehrig batted cleanup and wore number 4. After Gehrig's brilliant career ended in 1939, he became the first player to have his number retired. This meant that no one on the Yankees—not even the coaches or manager—could ever wear it again. By the time the Yanks retired Ruth's number nine years later, the tradition was spreading throughout baseball and to other sports.

Players now get to choose their numbers, but two team-mates can't wear the same number simultaneously. In 1993 this caused quite a problem for Rickey Henderson, who had to give up his beloved number 24 when he was traded to the Blue Jays because Turner Ward was already wearing it. Before long, the slumping Henderson complained that he couldn't hit well with his new number, and he paid Ward $25,000 to give up his old one. Not all players are that inflexible. Mets *utilityman* Joe McEwing had been wearing number 47 for four seasons when another number 47 signed with the team in 2003: future Hall-of-Fame pitcher Tom Glavine, who'd worn the number for 15 years in Atlanta. In this case, the easygoing McEwing gave his number to the *veteran* and took number 11 (the total of the digits of his former number).

There's usually a reason behind the players' selections. Pitcher David Wells, a huge fan of the Babe, couldn't wear number 3 when he signed with the Yankees, so he settled for number 33. First basemen love number 17 because the slick-fielding Keith Hernandez wore it. Many players have honored Jackie Robinson by wearing number 42, but it's now off limits—in 1997 Major League Baseball celebrated the 50th anniversary of Robinson's breaking the color barrier by permanently retiring his number, although the few players already wearing it got to keep it: Butch Huskey, Mike Jackson, Scott Karl, Jose Lima, Mariano Rivera, and Mo Vaughn.

Some guys pick their numbers for more unusual reasons. Turk Wendell had such an intense love affair with number 99 (Charlie Sheen's character's number in the movie *Major League*) that his salary with the Mets ended in 99 cents, and he wore the number on his back—until he pitched poorly after his trade to the Phillies and switched to number 13. Sid Fernandez and Benny Agbayani wore number 50 because they're from Hawaii, the 50th state. Omar Olivares's number 00 made him the only player to wear his initials. Carlos May, born on May 17, 1948, switched to number 17 to become the first player to wear his birth date. Hall of Famer Carlton Fisk switched from number 27 to 72 upon his 1981 trade to the White Sox to represent the turnaround in his career. Catcher Todd Hundley chose number 9 because his father, Randy, wore the number during his career, but Todd eventually switched to number 09 so the strap that held his chest protector could fit neatly between the digits.

For a list of the greatest players and managers—past and present—and their uniform numbers, see appendix B on page 246.

CHEATING

Sometimes it's hard to tell the difference between cheating and just being a little sneaky. In baseball there are many examples of each, and some are so creative that the perpetrators practically deserve an award.

Pitchers occasionally hide emery boards in their sleeves, Vaseline under their caps, pine tar in their gloves, and anything else they can use to alter the surface—and therefore the flight—of the ball. As a member of the Los Angeles Dodgers, Hall-of-Fame pitcher Don Sutton used to cut the ball with a razor blade that he concealed in the heel of his glove. When other teams became suspicious, shortstop Maury Wills kept the blade and used it before tossing Sutton the ball at the start of the inning. One time Sutton was visited on the mound by an umpire who thought he saw something incriminating in the right-hander's glove. Instead, he found a note that read: "You're getting warm, but it's not here."

Catchers sometimes scuff the balls by grinding them into the dirt or swiping them against a hard piece of their equipment. Yankees catcher Yogi Berra did this for Whitey Ford, and they're both in the Hall of Fame. "I didn't begin cheating until late in my career, when I needed something to help me survive," said Ford. "I didn't cheat when I won the 25 games in 1961. I don't want anybody to get any ideas and take my Cy Young Award away. And I didn't cheat in 1963 when I won 24 games. Well, maybe a little."

Home teams, responsible for providing the balls, have been known to keep a few in a refrigerator and then give them to the ump when the other team is batting. (A cold ball becomes hard, loses its spring, and doesn't travel as far.) But the balls must be removed from the fridge at the right time so the *cowhide* returns to a normal temperature.

Hitters, in addition to taking steroids, can gain an illegal advantage by corking their bats. First, they drill an inch-wide hole from the end of the bat into the barrel. Then they replace the dense wood with lighter cork and plug the hole to conceal the operation. The cork not only makes the bat lighter (which increases bat speed) but prevents it from sounding hollow on contact. Long after winning the 1961 AL batting title, Tigers first baseman Norm Cash admitted using a corked bat. But many players have gotten caught in the act and faced one- to two-week suspensions, most notably Cubs outfielder Sammy Sosa, who in 2003 broke his corked bat and sent the contents flying. (He quickly admitted that he sometimes used a corked bat in batting practice to entertain the fans with longer home runs, but claimed that he accidentally used his practice bat during the game. Riiiiiight.) Cork isn't the only substance that can do the trick; Yankees third baseman Graig Nettles got busted in 1974 when his bat shattered and released a bunch of colorful Super Balls.

A historic case of dishonesty unfolded 50 years after New York Giants third baseman Bobby Thomson hit a dramatic three-run homer to send his team to the 1951 World Series. Evidence suggests that his manager, Leo Durocher, paid someone to sit in the center-field bleachers with binoculars and steal the catcher's signs. Other stories have surfaced about two members of the Giants who stole the signs from the team's center-field clubhouse (483 feet from home plate) and relayed them via a secret buzzer to the bullpen, where they were then passed to the hitters.

Baseball's rule book doesn't specify that sign-stealing is illegal. In fact, it's such a recognized part of the game that teams constantly go out of their way to disguise their signs. Who cares if they're stolen by the runner on second or a *clubby* or a fan in the bleachers? Thomson has denied getting the sign, but even if he did, he still had to hit the ball.

ATTENDANCE

Ever wonder why the box score says there were 40,565 people at the game when you're sure you saw that many empty seats? It's because "attendance" measures tickets sold, not the number of people who pass through the turnstiles. You'll notice a bigger discrepancy on rainy days.

LET IT RAIN

When bad weather forces everyone to go home early, the game still counts if it lasts at least five innings. But if the home team has the lead, the game can end after the top of the fifth because *last licks* apply to the final inning, whether it's before or after the ninth. If the game doesn't last five innings, the whole thing has to be replayed.

When rain is in the forecast, the team with the lead swings at first pitches and throws more strikes in order to reach the sixth inning quickly and make the game official. Meanwhile, the trailing team stalls by going deep into counts, stepping out of the batter's box between pitches, making extra pick-off throws, and needlessly changing pitchers. If the game is tied, both teams either swing for the fences or play *small ball,* a style of play in which basic fundamentals and simple strategies help advance runners one or two bases at a time but reduce the chance of a big inning.

THE SEVENTH-INNING STRETCH

On Opening Day in 1910, William Howard Taft, the 27th president of the United States, was at Griffith Stadium to watch the Washington Senators battle the Philadelphia Athletics. As the afternoon wore on, the 300-pound Taft became uncomfortable in his tiny wooden seat and finally stood up to stretch. The fans stood too, thinking the president was leaving—but he wasn't going anywhere and soon sat down. So did everyone else. It was the middle of the seventh inning, and a tradition was born.[4]

Two years earlier, Jack Norworth had written an instant hit song called "Take Me Out to the Ball Game," but it wasn't until 1971 that Hall-of-Fame announcer Harry Caray, then with the White Sox, became the first to sing it at a game.

---

[4]Incidentally, Taft started another tradition that day. After the introduction of the managers, the umpire handed him the ball and asked him to throw it over home plate. Since then, every president except Jimmy Carter has opened at least one season with a ceremonial first pitch.

Bam! Another tradition. Today fans in almost every major league stadium sing it during the seventh-inning stretch.

SUPERSTITIONS

When the pitcher has a no-hitter going, don't mention it. It's bad luck. You'll jinx him. That's all there is to it. Every player knows this. Even some announcers avoid saying it. In fact, it's bad luck for me to be writing about it, so I'm going to end this paragraph.

Baseball players are weird. They have funky habits and routines, bizarre superstitions and compulsions. They sleep with their bats to end slumps. They don't step on the foul lines between innings. They don't walk between the catcher and umpire when coming to bat. And that's just the beginning.

No matter how odd it gets, other players accept it. As fans, we must too. So don't judge infielder Tim Flannery, who said after his 18-game hitting streak ended in 1980, "I'm superstitious. Every night after I got a hit I ate Tex-Mex food and drank tequila. I had to stop hitting or die."

More examples? Outfielder Lenny Dykstra threw out his batting gloves after every at-bat in which he failed to get a hit. Manager Gene Mauch never washed his underwear, T-shirt, or uniform after his team won. Pitcher Turk Wendell used to brush his teeth and chew licorice between innings.

Then there was Wade Boggs, quite possibly the most superstitious player ever. He woke up at the same time every morning, took exactly 150 grounders during infield practice, ate chicken before every game (earning himself the nickname "Chicken Man"), and drew a chai, the Hebrew symbol for life, in the batter's box before each at-bat (and he's not Jewish). Before night games, he always began batting practice at 5:17 P.M. and his wind sprints at 7:17 P.M. to increase his chance of going 7-for-7. (A scoreboard operator in Toronto once tried to mess him up by flipping the clock directly from 7:16 to 7:18.) Was Boggs crazy? Obviously not. He batted .328 for his career, won five batting titles, collected more than 3,000 hits, played in 12 straight All-Star Games, won a World Series, and got inducted to the Hall of Fame.

But there are skeptics.

"For five years in the Minor Leagues," said outfielder Dusty Baker, "I wore the same underwear and still hit .250, so, no, I don't believe in that stuff."

DOUBLE SWITCH

When the manager makes a defensive change at the same time as a pitching change, it's called a double switch. It allows him to place the new players in either slot in the batting order, therefore delaying the pitcher's turn at bat. For example, if the seventh hitter ended the previous inning, the manager can remove him and the pitcher, insert the new position player in the ninth slot, and make the new pitcher bat seventh so he won't have to take his hacks until the team makes it all the way through the lineup.

THE MAGIC NUMBER

The magic number indicates how many wins (by the first-place team) and losses (by the second-place team) it'll take for a first-place team to reach the playoffs. Here's how to calculate it:

1. Figure out how many games remain for the first-place team.

2. Add one.

3. Subtract the number of games by which it leads the second-place team in the loss column.

Eh?

Let's say your favorite team is in first place with a record of 74-57 and has 31 games left in the 162-game schedule. You add 1 and get 32. If the second-place team is 68-61, it has lost 4 more games than your team, so you subtract 4 and get 28. There's your magic number. (If you want to keep track of it for the rest of the season, get 29 pieces of paper, number them 0 through 28, and stick them on the wall. Every time your team wins, tear down the biggest number. Every time the second-place team loses, remove another. When you see "0," it's time to celebrate.)

ROSTERS, TRANSACTIONS, AND CONTRACTS

Of all the things that make baseball unique, the one that most fans overlook is the beautiful complexity of balancing rosters, making transactions, and signing contracts. This is the true guts of the game, and the stuff that determines who you see on the field.

A team can't carry more than 25 players until September 1, when the limit increases to 40 for the remainder of the regular season; any time a guy is added to the roster, someone else must be removed. Players, therefore, are regularly *optioned* to and *recalled* from the minors, placed on and *activated* from the *disabled list* (*DL*), and traded or released. When placed on the DL, a player must remain out of action for either 15 or 60 days (depending on the severity of the injury), and his spot on the

roster opens for a temporary replacement. If a good player suf-
fers a minor injury, his team faces a dilemma: Put him on the
DL and use a substitute? Or list him as day-to-day and play
with only 24 men in case he quickly recovers?

Although teams can make trades anytime, there's a flurry of
transactions before each of the two *trading deadlines*. Until
4:00 P.M. EDT on July 31, a team can trade a player without
placing him on *waivers*. When he's on waivers, any other team
can claim him—and his salary. If his team simply wants to
gauge trade interest and possibly hold on to him, it places him
on revocable waivers. If his team definitely wants to dump
him, it places him on irrevocable waivers. Then, if nobody
claims him, the team can skip some of the contractual hurdles
in trading or sending him to the minors. After August 31, players who switch teams or join the expanded 40-man rosters
can't play in the postseason. As a result, struggling teams often
abandon the current season by trading superstars (and their
mega-salaries) to postseason contenders for prospects.

Teams' executives stay busy after the season; by November
20, they must protect certain major and minor league players
on the 40-man roster to prevent other teams from picking
them in the *Rule 5 Draft,* an annual off-season draft of players who are already in the Minor Leagues. Because many
farmhands are left unprotected, there are two rules that discourage other teams from snatching them:

- It costs $50,000 to select a player.

- A team that selects a player must either keep him on its
  major league roster for the entire following season or
  offer him back to his original team for only $25,000.

Usually, Rule 5 Draft picks don't end up making a huge
impact in the Major Leagues—if they're that good, they'd be

protected—but future stars have occasionally slipped through the cracks: 1987 American League MVP George Bell, two-time Cy Young Award winner Johan Santana, all-time saves leader Trevor Hoffman, and Hall-of-Fame outfielder Roberto Clemente.

Players prefer to sign multi-year deals because the money is guaranteed even if they start to suck. But teams prefer to avoid getting trapped by monster contracts. The result is frequent tension between management, players, agents, and even the fans, especially when negotiations spill into the season. When a team and player absolutely cannot agree on the terms of a contract, they go to *arbitration*—the use of a third party to settle a salary dispute.

Long after signing a player, the team might decide that it doesn't want him. If he has a no-trade clause in his contract, the team is stuck with him. (So-called *10/5 players* can veto any trade. They're the guys who've been in the majors for at least 10 years and played for 5 consecutive seasons with their current team.) Otherwise, the general manager can try to make a trade, but he might struggle to find another team willing to take on the player's enormous salary. If the player becomes so lousy that he has absolutely no value, his team will simply release him. But don't feel bad for the guy. He still gets paid for the remainder of his contract, as do managers who get fired midseason and players who miss time because of baseball-related injuries.[5] Albert Belle, whose arthritic hip forced his

---

[5] If players get hurt off the field, they can lose money; certain activities are banned by their contracts. During Spring Training in 2002, Giants second baseman Jeff Kent broke his wrist while performing tricks on his motorcycle, but told general manager Brian Sabean that he'd fallen while washing his truck. Kent was publicly ridiculed when the truth came out, though he healed quickly and still got paid. Two winters later, Yankees third baseman Aaron Boone tore a ligament in his knee

abrupt retirement after the 2000 season, not only collected the $39 million that the Orioles owed him through 2003 but continued to receive meal money when the team was on the road.

FREE AT LAST

In the old days, owners had total control of players. Salaries stayed low, and guys couldn't change teams. There simply was no bargaining—that is, until 1966, when Marvin Miller, the chief negotiator for the United Steelworkers Union, was hired to run the Major League Baseball Players Association (otherwise known as the players' union).

The following year, Miller visited every team during Spring Training, where he earned the players' support and convinced them to stick together. This solidarity, along with Miller's successful court battles and hard-nosed tactics, brought players their first significant salary increase in two decades by forcing owners to share more money from licensing and broadcasting revenues. Miller also improved conditions for the players by demanding padded outfield walls, better warning tracks, safer locker rooms, and more sensible schedules.

His biggest accomplishment was getting players the right to accept contract offers from teams other than those that originally signed them. It was called free agency, and Hall-of-Fame pitcher Catfish Hunter signed the first free agent contract (with—surprise!—George Steinbrenner's Yankees) in

---

while playing basketball—another commonly banned activity. When he fessed up about his injury, the Yankees voided his $5.75 million contract and released him, but he still collected 30 days of termination pay worth $917,553. (No word on whether Mariners outfielder Ken Griffey Jr. got paid for the game he missed after his protective cup slipped out of place and pinched his testicle. True story.)

December 1974. Suddenly, owners had to outbid each other to sign star players, and salaries shot up:

BASEBALL'S AVERAGE SALARY

1970—$29,303

1975—$44,676

1980—$143,756

1985—$371,571

1990—$578,930

1995—$1,071,029

2000—$1,998,034

2005—$2,632,655

2010—yikes

Although economic inflation is partially responsible, many people blame Miller for these out-of-control numbers and forget to give him credit for being an innovator, a strong negotiator, and a passionate baseball fan whose work inspired and helped professional athletes in other sports.

CONTROVERSIAL ISSUES

Like anything else, baseball has experienced its ups and downs. Here are the biggest issues and ugliest moments in the history of the sport.

THE BLACK SOX—In 1919 several players on the White Sox accepted money from gamblers and intentionally lost the

World Series to the Reds. Baseball commissioner Kenesaw Mountain Landis responded by banning eight of them for life, including the popular "Shoeless" Joe Jackson, whom many feel played his best and was wrongly accused. The 1919 World Series became known as the Black Sox Scandal and nearly destroyed the public's faith in the sport. Luckily, there was a young player emerging as a star, who made headlines with his *tape-measure home runs* and drew fans back to the ballparks. His name was Babe Ruth.

PETE ROSE—While managing the Reds after his playing days, Pete Rose got busted for baseball's biggest sin: gambling. Even though he put money on his own team, it was a serious violation because he could have overused certain pitchers on certain days and risked their careers for his own gain. Commissioner Bart Giamatti banned him for life in 1989, and Rose, despite insisting he hadn't gambled, accepted his punishment at the time. Fifteen years later, he admitted he gambled, hoping that commissioner Bud Selig would overturn the ban and allow him to be inducted to the Hall of Fame.

He hasn't.

Everyone agrees that Rose's stats are worthy of the Hall, but many people feel that his lack of integrity should keep him out. (Of course, no one seems to care that Ty Cobb, a known racist, is in the Hall.)

BEANBALLS—Don Drysdale once said, "The pitcher has to find out if the hitter is timid, and if the hitter is timid, he has to remind the hitter he's timid." Bob Gibson famously claimed that he'd throw at his own mother if she crowded the plate. While these attitudes may seem a bit harsh, no one blamed these guys for throwing inside because eventually they had to step into the batter's box and face retaliation. But when the

AL adopted the designated hitter rule in 1973, tempers flared when teams suddenly had no way to get even with an aggressive pitcher. Sure, they could bean one of his undeserving teammates or take out a middle infielder with a nasty slide, but there was no way of guaranteeing revenge. As a result, today's hypersensitive players are quick to *charge the mound*.[6] Umpires, given the tough job of preventing brawls, have been quick to issue warnings after the first sign of ill will.

So what's the problem?

If either pitcher throws inside with "intent" after a warning, both he and his manager get ejected. This leaves pitchers reluctant to throw inside and enables batters—fear factor gone—to lunge over the plate and reach pitches on the outside corner. (And some people wonder why offense is increasing.)

SKEWED STATS—Just as the 162-game season gives current players a statistical edge over old-timers, who played 154-game schedules, a similar change has skewed postseason statistics: the addition of the Division and League Championship Series. Here's an example. In 1964 Yankees outfielder Mickey Mantle hit his 18th career postseason home run to establish a new record. In 2003 another Yankees outfielder, Bernie Williams, passed him. Mantle hit all his homers in the World Series, but Williams (who also holds the career postseason RBI record) had extra opportunities. Who's better? Who knows.

JUICED BALLS—After pitchers had dominated the sport for several decades, the number of home runs inexplicably surged in 1987. Major League Baseball officials were accused of secretly "juicing" the balls—in other words, instructing Rawlings employees to stitch the balls tighter so they'd travel

---

[6]In 1994 Reds outfielder Reggie Sanders charged Expos pitcher Pedro Martinez after being hit by an 0-2 pitch in the eighth inning of a perfect game!

farther and satisfy homer-hungry fans. When MLB denied it, several pitchers dissected balls and discovered that the new rubber cores did indeed bounce higher than the old ones. Aha! But were the old balls manufactured differently, or were they just, well, old?

STEROIDS—Forget juiced balls. The problem is juiced muscles. When Mark McGwire shattered Roger Maris's single-season home run record in 1998, he was using androstenedione, an over-the-counter supplement that helps the body produce testosterone. "Andro" was already banned by many other sports, but it was legal in baseball until 2004. That's when several of the sport's biggest stars—Gary Sheffield, Jason Giambi, and Barry Bonds—got caught up in a steroid scandal and testified before a grand jury about their connection to the Bay Area Laboratory Co-Operative (BALCO), the company that had provided steroids to them. The testimony was leaked to the media, and the whole world learned that all three had admitted using steroids (although Bonds and Sheffield claimed they didn't know it). This, combined with mounting pressure from the U.S. government to clean up the game, finally prompted the players' union and MLB to agree on a stricter testing policy and a longer list of banned substances. For the first time, players would be tested randomly and face disciplinary action for their first offense: a 10-day suspension without pay. Second-time offenders would miss 30 days, third-time offenders 60, and fourth-time offenders—not that anyone would be dumb enough to get caught that many times—a full year.

The government backed off in 2005—until Jose Canseco, a former MVP and admitted steroid-user, published a tell-all book about players who supposedly cheated and the baseball execs who allegedly looked the other way. Congress launched an investigation and held a special hearing, months before Rafael Palmeiro, a prolific slugger who had just joined the exclusive 3,000-hit club, tested positive for the newly banned stanozolol.

The controversy erupted. Again.

By the end of the year, with the government making fresh threats to intervene, MLB and the players' union agreed on stiffer penalties: a 50-game suspension for the first offense, 100 games for the second, and a lifetime ban for the third. Although new scandals and accusations made headlines in 2006, only two Major Leaguers tested positive.

GOING ON STRIKE—Major League Baseball has endured eight work stoppages since 1972, most of which were resolved before the regular season, but there have been two big ones. In 1981 a 50-day strike split the season and forced the first-half and second-half winners to face each other in *October*. (Marvin Miller organized that one.) In 1994 a 232-day strike wiped out the World Series and lasted into the next season. The disputes alienated millions of fans, but there were serious issues that needed—and still need—to be resolved, most importantly, the lack of a competitive balance. In other sports, there's a limit on how much teams can pay players. It's called a *salary cap*, and baseball doesn't have one. Instead, MLB uses an annual *luxury tax* to penalize the few teams whose payrolls exceed a predetermined level.[7] Unfortunately,

---

[7] As that level rose to $128 million in 2005, the Yankees ($213.1 million) became the first team in baseball history to break $200 million. Because it was the third straight year that the Yanks had exceeded the level, they had to pay the maximum 40 percent of the difference—or $34 million—to the Office of the Commissioner. Meanwhile, the Red Sox ($141.9 million) were the only other team that had to pay the tax, and neither they nor the Yankees made it past the first round of the playoffs.

the tax hasn't deterred overspending, and as a result, *small-market teams* still can't compete with wealthy franchises because they don't generate enough money to sign—or keep—star players.

CONTRACTION—Many owners complain about losing money. One proposed solution is *contraction*. With fewer teams, there'd be a better concentration of talent. The level of play would increase. Games would be more fun to watch. There'd be more fans per team, and presto! the financial burden would ease. But who deserves to get booted? The players say no one; one less team means 25 fewer jobs, so the union is fighting it. And don't forget the hundreds of stadium employees who'd lose their jobs, as well as the neighborhood hotels and restaurants and stores that would lose business.

YAWN—Many people love that baseball is untimed. But no fan is happy when a game is already three hours old in the seventh inning, and the *human rain delay* steps out of the box between pitches to obsessively adjust his batting gloves after there have been back-to-back pitching changes and five consecutive pick-off throws. After the 2000 season, in which the average game lasted nearly three hours, Bud Selig took action. He forced hitters to have an extra bat ready in case one breaks. He told managers to signal for a relief pitcher before crossing the foul line on the way to the mound. He instructed umpires to call a ball if the pitcher takes more than 12 seconds between pitches. He demanded that new innings start on time after the intended two-minute-and-five-second commercial break. These were great ideas. Ready for the lousy ones that Selig scrapped after a brief trial? He told batters not to step out of the batter's box. (For some, stepping out is a deliberate attempt to disrupt the pitcher's rhythm.) He ranked home-plate umpires according to pitch counts in order to encourage them to call more strikes. (This caused a predictable uproar.) He even wanted to ditch the intentional walk process and immediately award the batter first base. (Ever seen a wild pitch on an intentional walk? It happens.) Baseball is still slow, but let's give Selig some credit: from 2001 to 2003, he shaved 12 minutes off the average game.

UMPS VERSUS MLB—In addition to QuesTec and pitch count rankings, umpires have clashed with baseball officials on many occasions. In 1999 the relationship got so bad that 22 umps, backed by their union, joined forces in a mass resignation as their new contract negotiations approached. But the baseball officials shocked them by accepting their resignations and finding replacements. Since then, several umpires have been rehired, while others have filed lawsuits. So when you're yelling at the umps for being blind and stupid, that's the least of their concerns.

CHAPTER 10
RANDOM STUFF TO NOTICE

You can observe a lot by watching.

—Yogi Berra, Hall-of-Fame catcher

ALWAYS CHEWING

Baseball involves lots of waiting. Players, whether sitting on the bench or standing in the field, need to entertain themselves, so they chew. And chew. And chew.

Teams provide bubble gum and sunflower seeds—true ballplayers put a handful in their mouth and crack open the shells one by one—but nearly one-third of major leaguers choose smokeless tobacco over the free stuff, so they spit. And spit. And spit. (Some guys don't chew anything, but still spit. It's part of baseball's culture.)

You can spot the guys who *dip* by looking for their bulging lower lips or the outline of a puck-shaped can of tobacco in their back pockets. But don't waste your time looking in the minors, where tobacco was banned in 1993.

READ MY LIPS

Manager-umpire arguments provide an excellent opportunity for you to practice lip-reading. Not only can you pick out four-letter words ("balk" and "safe," for example), but you might recognize an entire phrase, like "under the tag" or "I beg to differ."

At some point in the game, you'll probably get another chance to lip-read when the pitcher walks toward the dugout after a rough inning. But if he covers his mouth with his glove, you'll have to settle for watching the fielders yell, "I got it!"

GET DIRTY

Players are always fidgeting with the dirt. Here are the reasons why:

- The hitter digs a small hole at the back of the batter's box so he can put his foot in it and push off as he steps into the pitch. If dirt sticks to his shoes, he taps it off with his bat.

- The pitcher digs a hole in front of the rubber so he can push off harder on his deliveries. He also fills in the other pitcher's *landing spot* if it's messing him up. If dirt sticks to his shoes, he scrapes them on a small bed of spikes embedded in the back of the mound or picks out the clumps with an emery board.

- An infielder taps and kicks the dirt to smooth it out and prevent bad hops. If his throwing hand becomes sweaty, he wipes it in the dirt to dry his skin so he'll be able to get a good grip on the ball.

- A base runner fusses with the dirt to improve his footing and get a good jump. When he dives head-first, his belt buckle collects dirt, so he calls time and carefully jiggles it to avoid getting any in his pants.

MUSIC

The home team can blast music between pitches, batters, and innings, but never while the ball is in play. Sometimes the tunes relate to what has just happened on the field. For example, you might hear "Wild Thing" after a walk and "Another One Bites the Dust" when the visiting team's manager makes a pitching change.

Home-team hitters select their pre-at-bat music and often stick with the same song for weeks, months, or years. Why do they always choose rock, rap, or salsa? Presumably, baseball players don't listen to show tunes—or perhaps they just don't want to admit it.

THE SOUNDS OF THE GAME

Stop talking and turn up the volume. There's a lot you can hear:

- Some pitchers grunt as they push off the rubber.
- The home-plate ump sometimes says why the pitch missed the strike zone, for example, "That's inside! Two-and-two."
- Restless fans yell, "Balk!" at the visiting team's pitcher even when he legally fakes a pick-off throw.
- The batter might yelp in pain when he gets beaned.
- When the first baseman fields a grounder in the hole, his teammate or coach shouts, "Get over!" to remind the pitcher to cover.
- Microphones attached to the bases sometimes let you hear the runners sliding.
- When the batter hits a potential sac fly, the third-base coach yells, "Tag!" to remind the runner to return to the base.

- Kids in the crowd scream, "Heeere!! Heeere!!" whenever a ball boy or coach retrieves a loose ball.

- Fans constantly cheer and boo. (You know this because you're one of them.) When they make noise for a guy with an "oo" sound in his name (like Kevin Youkilis or Mike Mussina), it's hard to tell the difference. Sometimes, the crowd makes noise for the fan who catches—or drops—a foul ball.

- Players curse more than you can imagine. Obviously, the networks try to hide it, but some words slip through.

THE ANNOUNCERS

Some announcers use the same phrase every time a certain play takes place. Chris Berman says, "Back-back-back-back-back-back-back," on home runs. John Sterling declares, "Thuhhhhhh Yankees win!" after the final out. Both Harry Caray and Phil Rizzuto made "Holy cow!" famous. Listen for other catchy phrases, and you'll be able to imitate the men behind the mikes.

Of course, even the best announcers aren't perfect. Not only do they discuss the answers to the trivia questions before you've had a chance to think, but they might mispronounce players' names, mix up the left and right fielders, and forget that the manager has made a substitution. When you notice it, take pride in knowing something they didn't.

AROUND THE HORN

Have you noticed that the catcher doesn't always throw the ball back to the pitcher after a strikeout? Or where the first baseman chucks the ball after a groundout? When there's no one on base, the infielders toss the ball *around the horn* to keep their arms loose and their minds fresh. The ball's path depends on where the out was made. How many different patterns can you find?

STAYING INFORMED

At the game, the scoreboard tells you what you need to know. At home, a tiny box of graphics on your screen does the job. Every network has its own style. Here's one example:

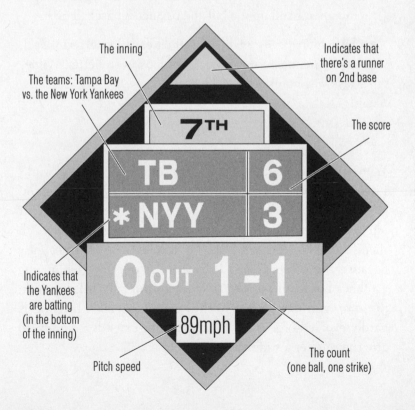

The inning

Indicates that there's a runner on 2nd base

The teams: Tampa Bay vs. the New York Yankees

7ᵀᴴ

The score

TB   6

*NYY   3

Indicates that the Yankees are batting (in the bottom of the inning)

0 OUT 1 - 1

89mph

Pitch speed

The count (one ball, one strike)

CAPS

Here are three lesser-known facts about baseball caps:

- Almost every player writes his name or uniform number underneath the bill, or at least on the inside. This helps his teammates identify it (along with his glove) so they can bring it to him when he gets left on base after the third out.

- When the home team needs to put up a *crooked number,* fans wear their caps creatively for good luck. These are called *rally caps,* and the easiest way to make one is to turn it inside out. Some people fold their caps and wear them on one side of their head, while the most daring rally cap craftsmen bend up the bill and balance a baseball on it.

- Outfielders occasionally wear their caps loosely so they'll fly off and make running catches look even better. Willie Mays was notorious for the practice.

IBB

Who calls for an intentional walk and how does it work? First, the manager of the team in the field flashes four fingers, which is the universal sign. Then the pitcher lobs four pitches far enough from the plate so the batter can't reach them, but close enough that his catcher can. It's not easy because the catcher must keep at least one foot within the catcher's box until the pitcher releases the ball. If he doesn't, the ump will charge him with a catcher's balk (this rule is hardly ever enforced), so he stands and extends one arm to give the pitcher a wide target.

WARM-UP PITCHES

The pitcher's arm is so delicate that it earns him special privileges, like playing catch (to stay loose) with an infielder during a brief delay and wearing his jacket (to stay warm) when running the bases. But when he takes the mound after an inning break or pitching change, he faces a strict limit of eight warm-up pitches—unless he replaces a pitcher who got injured or ejected, and then he can throw as long as he wants. Either way, he tells his catcher what to expect by using a standard set of gestures with his glove:

- **Fastball**—He starts with the tip of his glove facing down and flicks it up and away from his body, as if shooing a fly.

- **Curveball**—He points the tip of his glove up, palm facing his chest, and flips it out and down.

- **Slider**—He moves his glove to one side with a backhand motion.

- **Change-up**—Palm facing down, he jabs the tip of his glove toward home plate and quickly pulls it back.

- **Splitter**—Palm facing down, he flings the tip of his glove toward the ground.

- **Knuckleball**—Palm facing down, he shakes his glove.

Before his final warm-up pitch, he flicks the glove over his shoulder to remind the catcher to throw through. Then, if there's a base runner and he still isn't loose, he can make a few extra pick-off throws.

THE FIRST BASEMAN'S BALL

Ever notice that the first baseman catches a ball as he heads back to the dugout after the third out? It's the infielders' warm-up ball. The first-base coach holds it once the inning gets started.

NEW BALL

Whether the pitcher doesn't like the way a particular ball feels (it might have flat seams or be too slick) or the batter fouls one into the stands, the umpire puts a new ball in play. Usually, he hands it to the catcher, but sometimes he throws it right to the pitcher. Watch out. Some umps have *cannons!*

ALERT FANS

Some fans are clueless. They think every routine fly ball is going to be a home run and every close play that goes against their team is a conspiracy by the umpires.

Some fans are alert. On the replay of a home run from a side angle, watch the people over the dugout. There's always one guy who instantly judges the flight of the ball and jumps up to cheer before everyone else.

Some fans are human. When a foul tip smacks the screen behind home plate, they flinch even though they're protected.

BLINKERS

Catchers are also human. Watch their eyes on slow-motion, close-up replays of the pitches coming in. They almost always blink.

REVERSE ANGLE

What would a beautiful left-handed swing look like from the right side? What if the batter ran to third base after hitting the ball? What if the catcher were left-handed? Watch a few minutes of the game in a mirror and you'll find out.

MUTE BUTTON

Ready for another weird way to watch the game? Mute your TV and turn on the radio broadcast. You'll have an image to go with all the jargon and fancy descriptions, and everything in this book will start to make sense sooner.

GLOSSARY: BASEBALL SLANG

The bases were drunk, and I painted the black with my best yakker. But blue squeezed me, and I went full. I came back with my heater, but the stick flares one the other way and chalk flies for two bases. Three earnies! Next thing I know, skipper hooks me and I'm sipping suds with the clubby.

—Ed Lynch, former major league pitcher

-A-

A-B-C ball—a style of play in which the offensive team uses basic fundamentals to advance its runners one or two bases at a time

A-ball—the third lowest of six levels in the Minor Leagues; often referred to as Single-A

ace—the best starting pitcher on the team

activate—to return an injured or suspended player to the roster

add and subtract—to throw pitches at different speeds

advance scout—a scout who travels ahead of the team and reports the strengths and weaknesses of future opponents

ahead in the count—at an advantage because of the number of balls and strikes

airmail—to throw the ball way too high

ALCS—American League Championship Series, the second of three rounds in the playoffs

ALDS—American League Division Series, the first of three rounds in the playoffs

all field/no hit—describes a player who fields well and hits poorly

All-Star break—the three-day midseason break for the All-Star Game

All-Star Game—the annual exhibition game between the best players in each league

alley—the space between outfielders

amateur draft—the First-Year Player Draft

appeal—a request, made by a fielder to an umpire, to call out a runner who left his base too soon or missed the base entirely

arbitration—the use of a third party to settle a salary dispute

Arizona Fall League—the 32-game instructional league to which major league teams send their top prospects

arm slot—the angle of the pitcher's arm as he releases the ball

around the horn—around the infield

aspirin tablet—a pitch thrown so fast that the ball looks like a little white speck

assist—a statistic awarded to a fielder who records an out by throwing the ball

asterisk—a symbol that indicates when a record or accomplishment was achieved dubiously

AstroTurf—an artificial playing surface, last used by the Blue Jays in 2004

at 'em ball—a line drive hit right at a fielder

atom ball—an at 'em ball

-B-

backdoor—describes an off-speed pitch (often a slider or curveball) that starts outside and moves over the edge of home plate at the last second

backstop—1. the wall behind home plate 2. the catcher

backup—describes an off-speed pitch (often a slider) that stays over the inside edge of home plate

bad ball hitter—a batter who's good at hitting pitches out of the strike zone

bad hop—an unexpected bounce

bag—a base

bail out—to fearfully step out of the way of a pitch, usually after getting tricked by the initial movement of a curveball

balk—an illegal movement by the pitcher that deceives a runner

Baltimore Chop—a batted ball that hits home plate (or the hard dirt near it) and bounces so high that the fielders don't have time to make a play

bandbox—a small ballpark that favors the hitters

bang-bang play—a very close play

barrel—the thickest part of the bat

base hit—a single

base knock—a base hit

base on balls—a walk

basement—last place

bases are drunk—bases loaded

bases empty—no runners on base

bases loaded—runners on every base

basket catch—a two-handed, waist-high catch with the palms turned up

bat around—to send every hitter in the lineup to bat in one inning

bat speed—the quickness of a hitter's swing

batter's eye—the dark backdrop beyond the center-field wall that helps the hitter see the ball as it leaves the pitcher's hand

battery—the pitcher and catcher

batting a thousand—describes a player with a perfect batting average

batting average—a statistic that shows how often the batter gets a hit

batting crown—batting title

batting title—the distinction of leading the league in batting average

BBWAA—Baseball Writers' Association of America

beanball—a pitch that hits the batter

beaned—hit by a pitch; sometimes used to mean hit in the head

beat out—to barely reach first base safely on a batted ball

bees in the hands—the stinging feeling after hitting the ball off the handle of the bat

behind in the count—at a disadvantage because of the number of balls and strikes

bender—a curveball

Bermuda Triangle—the area between the infielders and outfielders

big club—a major league team

big dance—the World Series

big fly—a home run

bite—1. to swing 2. the downward movement of a curveball

biter—a slider

blank—to shut out

bleeder—a softly batted ball that trickles through the infield or bloops just past it for a hit

bloop and a blast—a quick way to score two runs

blooper—1. a weak fly ball 2. a funny play often resulting in an error 3. an eephus

blue—a nickname for umpires (even though they no longer wear the color)

body armor—a batter's exceptionally large elbow guard

bonus baby—a player who receives a huge signing bonus after being selected early in the First-Year Player Draft

boot—to make an error

bow tie—a high, inside fastball

box score—a condensed, statistical recap of the game's action

BP—batting practice

BP fastball—a weak fastball in the middle of the strike zone

break the wrists—to swing past home plate on a check swing

breaking ball—a pitch that's slower than a fastball and drops as it reaches the batter

bring it—to throw hard

bring up—to promote a player from the Minor Leagues to the Major Leagues

brushback—an inside pitch that forces the batter to move quickly out of the way

bullpen—1. a team's relief pitchers 2. the area where the relievers warm up

bunt—to hold the bat over home plate and tap the ball gently

bush league—amateur play or behavior

butcher-boy—a batter who fakes a bunt, yanks the bat back into his regular hitting position, and tries to slap the ball past the drawn-in infielders

butterfly—a knuckleball

-C-

Cactus League—the league for Spring Training games in Arizona

Cadillac—to run leisurely

call time—to declare or request a time-out

call-up—a player who's promoted from the Minor Leagues to the Major Leagues

camp under it—to stand in the spot where a fly ball or pop-up will land

can of corn—a routine fly ball

cannon—a strong throwing arm

career year—a player's best season

carpet—AstroTurf or any other artificial playing surface

catbird seat—the hitter's advantage when he's ahead in the count

catcher's interference—an error on the catcher that's made by touching the batter or the bat during a swing

caught looking—called out on strikes

cellar—last place

chalk—the foul line

change-of-pace—a change-up

change-up—a pitch that's thrown slower than the fastball in order to make the batter swing too soon

charge the ball—to run forward and field the ball sooner

charge the mound—to run toward the pitcher to start a fight

cheat—to shade

check swing—a swing that the hitter tries to stop in midmotion

cheddar—cheese

cheese—exceptionally fast pitch speed

chin music—a high, inside fastball

choke up—to hold the bat an inch or two from the knob at the end of the handle

chuck-n-duck—describes a pitcher who's so bad that he might as well duck after he throws the ball

circle-change—a type of change-up

circus catch—an incredible catch

Class A—the third lowest of six levels in the Minor Leagues; often referred to as Single-A

Class A Advanced—the third highest of six levels in the Minor Leagues

Class A Short-Season—the second lowest of six levels in the Minor Leagues; like the Rookie level below it, the schedule runs from June to September

cleanup hitter—the fourth batter in the lineup, who can clean the bases with a grand slam if the first three guys get on base

clear the pitcher's slot—to reach base ahead of the pitcher with two outs

clicker—a small handheld device used by coaches to count the number of pitches thrown and by home-plate umpires to keep track of balls and strikes

climb the ladder—1. to swing at a high fastball 2. to throw a pitch higher than the one before

clock—to measure the speed of a pitch

closer—the final relief pitcher who tries to preserve the lead

closer by committee—a system in which the manager uses various pitchers to finish games

clothesline—a ball moving at such a high velocity that it travels parallel to the ground

clubby—a clubhouse attendant

clutch hit—a crucial hit in a tight situation

come-backer—a ground ball to the pitcher

command—a pitcher's ability not only to throw strikes but to hit the catcher's target within the strike zone

complete game—a game that the starting pitcher finishes

contact hitter—a batter who rarely strikes out

contraction—the elimination of teams from the Major Leagues

cookie—a pitch that's easy to hit

Cooperstown—the town where the Hall of Fame is located

count, the—the number of balls and strikes

country hardball—a style of play that's dominated by muscle and devoid of finesse

courtesy trot—an outfielder's perfunctory jog toward the wall on a long home run; he spares his pitcher some embarrassment by making it look like there was a chance to catch the ball

cowhide—the material used for the surface of the ball

crew chief—the head umpire

crooked number—any number of runs above "1"

cross hairs—the middle of the strike zone

cross-seam fastball—a four-seam fastball

crossed up—confused about which pitch to expect

crow hop—a small jump-step used by an outfielder to gain momentum before throwing

crowd the plate—to stand close to home plate

cue shot—a soft ground ball that's hit off the end of the bat with lots of spin

cup of coffee—a brief appearance in the Major Leagues

Curse of the Bambino—the jinx that prevented the Red Sox from winning a World Series for 84 years after the team sold Babe Ruth (aka "The Bambino") to the Yankees in 1920

curveball—a pitch that curves and drops as it reaches the batter

cut fastball—a fastball that moves laterally—away from a righty if thrown by a righty—as it reaches the batter

cutoff man—an infielder who relays a throw from the outfield

cut-out—the dirt area surrounding a base on a field with artificial turf

cutter—a cut fastball

Cy Young Award—the annual award for the best pitcher in each league

-D-

dancer—a knuckleball

day-night doubleheader—an afternoon game and a night game in one day, each with a separate admission

day-to-day—not injured severely enough to be placed on the disabled list

daylight play—a type of pick-off move at second base

dead ball—a ball that is ruled "out of play," forcing the action to stop

dead fish—a change-up

dead red—a fastball

deadball era—the first two decades of the 20th century, when the balls were not nearly as springy and home runs had not yet begun to dominate the sport

decision—a win or loss for a pitcher

deek—to decoy the runner into thinking that the ball is somewhere else

defensive indifference—a decision made by the team in the field to allow a runner to advance on a stolen base attempt

delayed steal—a stolen base on which the runner takes off after the pitch

delivery—the motion of throwing a pitch

designated hitter—a hitter who bats in place of the pitcher and doesn't play defense

deuce—a curveball

dewdrop—an eephus

DH—a designated hitter

dial it up—to pitch or swing harder than usual

diamond—the infield

Diamond Dust—a sandlike material used by groundskeepers to absorb water on the infield dirt

dig in—to get ready in the batter's box

dinger—a home run

dip—to chew tobacco

disabled list—the list of injured players

dish—home plate

Division I—the highest level of collegiate sports

DL—the disabled list

doctored ball—a ball that has been tampered with or defaced

Double-A—the second highest of six levels in the Minor Leagues

double clutch—to hesitate before throwing because of indecision or a bad grip on the ball

double dip—a doubleheader

double play—a single play during which the fielding team records two outs

double-play ball—a ground ball that enables the defense to record two outs

double-play depth—a defensive alignment in which the middle infielders move forward and closer to second base in order to have a better chance of turning a double play

double steal—two stolen bases by two runners at the same time

double switch—a simultaneous pitching change and defensive change

doubled off—retired on a double play by not making it back to the base after the ball has been caught on a fly

doubleheader—two games in one day

down Broadway
down Main Street
down the chute } —through the middle of the strike zone
down the gut
down the pipe

drag bunt—a bunt on which a left-handed batter starts moving toward first base before the pitch reaches him

drilled—hit by a pitch

drop the hammer—to throw a curveball

ducks on the pond—runners on base

dying quail—a weak fly ball between the infielders and out-fielders

dynasty—a team that wins several World Series in a short span

-E-

E-6—error on the shortstop

earned run average—a statistic that shows how many earned runs a pitcher allows every nine innings

earned runs—runs that are the pitcher's fault (as opposed to unearned runs, which score because of his teammates' errors)

earnies—earned runs

eat the ball—to hold the ball instead of throwing it

eephus—an extremely rare trick pitch that's thrown with a very high arc

$8 taxi ride—a very long home run

Elias—the Elias Sports Bureau, a company that provides obscure statistics

emergency catcher—a player who can catch if his team's regular catchers are unavailable

emeryball—a now-illegal pitch that pitchers used to throw by scuffing the ball with a nail file

ERA—earned run average

even count—the same number of balls as strikes

even with the bag—next to the base

excuse-me hit—a hit produced by a check swing

expand the strike zone—to swing at (or intentionally throw) a pitch outside of the strike zone

expansion—the addition of teams to the Major Leagues

express—a fastball

extra-base hit—a double, triple, or home run

eye-black—a substance that players smear under their eyes to reduce the sun's glare

-F-

fadeaway—a screwball

Fall Classic—the World Series

fall off a table—describes a curveball that breaks sharply as it reaches the batter

fan—to strike out

fan interference—an interruption caused by a spectator who reaches out of the stands and touches the ball

fantasy baseball—a game in which fans simulate managing by drafting major league players and creating "fantasy" teams that compete against each other in various statistical categories

farm system—all the minor league teams affiliated with one major league team

farm team—a minor league team

farmhand—a minor league player

fastball—a pitch that travels fast and relatively straight

feed—a short throw that leads a fielder to the base

fielder's choice—a defensive play that retires a runner instead of the hitter

fielding average—a statistic that shows how often the fielder completes his plays without messing up

55-footer—a pitch that bounces in front of home plate

fight it off—to hit a foul ball on a difficult two-strike pitch

finesse pitcher—a pitcher who throws soft and has excellent control

fireballer—a pitcher who throws exceptionally fast

fireman—a late-inning relief pitcher

first movement—the beginning of the pitcher's delivery

First-Year Player Draft—the annual event during which major league teams select amateur players from high school and college

five o'clock hitter—a player who hits well during batting practice and struggles in games

5.5 hole—the space between the third baseman and shortstop

five-run homer—the unreachable goal of a batter who's foolishly trying to hit a homer when his team is losing by more than four runs

five-tool player—a player who can run fast, throw hard, field well, hit for power, and hit for a high batting average

flame-thrower—a pitcher who throws exceptionally fast

flash leather—to make a great defensive play

flip-downs—sunglasses with lenses that stay up until the fielder needs them, at which point he flips them down

floater—a knuckleball

flutterball—a knuckleball

folly floater—an eephus

force play—a play on which the runner is forced to run to the next base

forkball—a slower version of the split-finger fastball

fosh—a change-up

foul pole—the pole that separates fair and foul territory behind the outfield wall

foul tip—a foul ball that hardly changes direction because the bat barely touches it

four days' rest—the typical amount of time off between games for a starting pitcher

four-bagger—a home run

four-seam fastball—a type of fastball that's easy to control because it stays straight

four-seamer—a four-seam fastball

four-wheel drive—a home run

frame—1. an inning 2. to hold the mitt in place after catching a borderline strike in order to influence the umpire's call

free agent—a player who is eligible to sign a contract with any team

free pass—a base on balls

free-swinger—a batter who swings at most pitches

Frick Award—the award for announcers who get inducted into the Hall of Fame

frisbee—a very slow curveball

front office—the team executives who make the big decisions behind the scenes

frozen rope—an extremely hard line drive

full count—three balls, two strikes

fungo—a ball hit to a fielder during practice

-G-

gamer—1. a player's special bat or glove that he uses only in games 2. a hard-nosed player who battles through aches and pains and does whatever it takes to win

gap—the space between outfielders

gapper—a batted ball that lands between the outfielders

gas—a fastball

gassed—too tired to pitch effectively

get-away day—the last game of a series after which both teams travel to another city

get cheated—to fail to swing as hard as possible

get good wood on it—to hit the ball hard

get-me-over fastball—a weak fastball that the pitcher simply tries to throw for a strike when he's behind in the count

get the handle—to get a good grip on the ball

giddy-up—high pitch speed

glove-to-glove—the amount of time the catcher takes to catch a pitch and throw it to the middle infielder covering second on a stolen base attempt

go against the book—to make an unconventional strategic decision

go deep—to hit a home run

go fishing—to swing at a pitch that's out of the strike zone

go for the downs—to try to hit a home run

go the distance—to pitch a complete game

go the other way—to hit the ball to the opposite field

go yard—to hit a home run

Gold Glove Award—the annual award for the best fielder at each position in each league

Gold Glover—a player who wins the Gold Glove Award

golden sombrero—the dubious distinction of striking out four times in one game

good eye—good knowledge of the strike zone

goose egg—the number "0" on the scoreboard

gopher ball—a ball that's hit for a home run

gopheritis—the tendency to give up a lot of home runs

grand salami—a grand slam

grand slam—a home run with the bases loaded

granny—a grand slam

Grapefruit League—the league for Spring Training games in Florida

grass-cutter—a ground ball that takes so many bounces that it's almost rolling

green light—permission to steal a base or swing with three balls and no strikes

Green Monster—the 37-foot wall in left field at Fenway Park in Boston

groove the ball—to throw a pitch through the middle of the strike zone

ground-rule double—an automatic double, the result of a fair ball bouncing out of play or being touched by a fan

ground rules—the set of rules for each stadium that cover circumstances not mentioned in the standard rules

guess-hitter—a hitter who decides before the pitch is thrown whether he will swing

gun—1. a strong throwing arm 2. a radar gun (which measures pitch speed)

gyroball—a mysterious pitch that was recently invented by two Japanese scientists

-H-

hack—a swing

hammer—a curveball

hammy—a hamstring

hamstring—the muscle group in back of the thigh

handcuffed—unable to get the glove in position to catch the ball

hanger—a hanging curveball

hanging curveball—a curveball that's easy to hit because it stays up in the strike zone

happy zone—the location within the strike zone where the batter hits with most power

hat trick—the dubious distinction of striking out three times in one game

headhunter—a pitcher with a reputation for throwing at or near batters' heads

heater—a fastball

heavy ball—a pitch that seems to have extra momentum and therefore does not jump off the hitter's bat

heavy hitter—a batter who hits lots of home runs

hidden ball trick—a rare defensive play in which an infielder secretly keeps the ball after a pickoff throw or a conference on the mound so he can tag out the unsuspecting runner

hill—the pitcher's mound

hit-and-run—an offensive play in which the runner breaks for second base in order to pull the defense out of position and give the batter a better chance of getting a hit

hit behind the runner—to hit a ground ball to the right side so a runner on second can advance to third

hit for the cycle—to hit a single, double, triple, and home run in one game

hit it on the screws—to hit the ball extremely hard

hit it where it's pitched—to hit an outside pitch to the opposite field

hit it with the Sunday *Times*—to hit the ball softly, as if the bat were a rolled-up newspaper

hit the cutoff man—to throw the ball low so the infielder who makes the relay throw can catch it

hitch—a tendency of some hitters to drop and then quickly raise their hands right before swinging

hitter's park—a field that favors the offense because of its small dimensions

hitting streak—consecutive games with at least one hit

hold—a statistic awarded to a relief pitcher who records at least one out and preserves a small midgame lead

hold the runner on—to keep the runner close to the base by standing on it and waiting for a pick-off throw

Home Run Derby—the home run–hitting contest on the day before the All-Star Game

homestand—a series of games at a team's home ballpark

hook—a curveball

hook slide—a baserunning maneuver in which the runner slides past the base and hooks it with his back foot to avoid being tagged

horsehide—a nickname for the ball (even though the outer layer is now made of cowhide)

hosed—thrown out at a base

hot box—a rundown

hot corner—third base

hot stove—the off-season trades and free agent signings

hug the line—to stay close to the foul line

hugger—a ground ball that trickles just inside the foul line

human rain delay—a player who takes a long time to get ready between pitches

hummer—a fastball

hung out to dry—caught in between bases

hung up—caught in between bases

hustle double—a fairly ordinary hit that the batter turns into a double by running full speed right out of the batter's box

-I-

in a hole—behind in the count

in-between hop—a bounce that is hard to catch because it lands at an awkward distance from the fielder

in-betweener—an in-between hop

in play—in bounds or active

in the driver's seat—ahead in the count

in the hole—1. between two infielders 2. due to bat after the on-deck hitter

independent league—a league that's unaffiliated with Major League Baseball

indicator—a gesture that's used by a coach or player to validate or nullify the rest of his signs

infield fly rule—a rule that prevents the defense from taking advantage of the runners on a pop-up

infield in—a defensive alignment in which the infielders play closer to home plate to prevent a runner on third from scoring on a ground ball

inherited runners—runners on base when a relief pitcher enters the game

inside-out the ball—to hit an inside pitch to the opposite field

inside-the-park home run—a home run that stays within the playing field

instant replay—a slow-motion replay that helps referees (in other sports) make accurate decisions

insurance run—a run that widens a small lead

interleague—National League versus American League

-J-

jack—a home run

jam—1. to force the hitter to hit an inside pitch off the handle of the bat 2. a difficult situation for the pitcher

jam sandwich—a pitch that jams the hitter

jelly-legs—a hitter whose knees buckle when he gets fooled by a curveball

journeyman—a player who has frequently changed teams, possibly struggling to stay in the starting lineup or even in the Major Leagues

juice—steroids

jump—the first few steps when running the bases or chasing a batted ball

Junior Circuit—the American League (which became a major league in 1901, 25 years after the National League)

junkballer—a pitcher who throws lots of off-speed pitches

-K-

K—a strikeout

keep score—to document the game's action with specific written symbols and abbreviations

keystone—second base

kitchen—the area near the hitter's hands

knock—a hit

knockdown pitch—an inside pitch that forces the hitter to fall down while dodging it

knuckle-curve—a type of curveball

knuckleball—a pitch that flutters unpredictably

knuckler—a knuckleball

-L-

LaLob—an eephus

landing spot—the spot where the pitcher steps every time he throws the ball

last licks—the home team's opportunity to bat in the second half of the ninth inning (and in extra innings if necessary)

laugher—a game with a lopsided score

launching pad—a stadium where teams hit lots of home runs

lay one down—to bunt

lay out—to dive for the ball

lead runner—the runner who's closer to home plate

leadoff hitter—the first hitter

League Championship Series—the second of three rounds in the playoffs

League Division Series—the first of three rounds in the playoffs

leave the building—to hit a home run

leg it out—to run full speed and barely reach first base safely

letter-high—at the top of the strike zone

leverage—the height of the pitcher's release point

life—late movement on a pitch

lights out—unhittable

line drive in the box score—a humorous description of a soft base hit (because of how it looks to a person who didn't watch the game but will read about it the next day)

lip—the ridge where the infield dirt meets the outfield grass

lit up—describes a pitcher who gives up lots of hits

little ball—a style of play in which the offensive team uses basic fundamentals to advance its runners one or two bases at a time

local—an off-speed pitch

lollipop—a soft throw

long man—a long reliever

long reliever—a relief pitcher who often pitches for several innings

longball—a home run

long-toss—to play catch while standing as far apart as possible

Lord Charles—a dominant curveball

luxury tax—an annual fine for the few teams whose payrolls exceed a predetermined limit

-M-

magic number—a number that measures how close a first-place team is to reaching the postseason

major league pop-up—an incredibly high pop-up

makeup—attitude and baseball instincts

manufacture a run—to score a run with basic fundamentals instead of a big hit

meatball—a pitch that's easy to hit

Mendoza line—a .200 batting average, named after infielder Mario Mendoza, who finished below the mark five times in his nine-year career

merry-go-round—describes the infield when all three runners start running with two outs and a full count

middle infielders—the second baseman and shortstop

middle reliever—a relief pitcher who pitches during the middle of the game

middle-in—between the middle of the strike zone and the inside edge of home plate

Midsummer Classic—the All-Star Game

MiLB—Minor League Baseball

MLB—Major League Baseball

modern era—1893 to the present

moon shot—a high, long home run

mop up—to pitch in relief after another pitcher gives up a lot of runs

moth—a knuckleball

movement—the irregular flight of a pitch

Mr. Snappy—a curveball

mustard—high velocity on a thrown ball

MVP—most valuable player

-N-

napping—not paying attention

Negro Leagues—leagues for African-American players before the 1947 desegregation of Major League Baseball

neighborhood play—a force play in which the middle fielder comes close enough to touching second base that he gets the call from the umpire

nibble—to aim for the edges of the strike zone

nightcap—the second game of a doubleheader

90 feet—the distance from one base to the next

NLCS—National League Championship Series, the second of three rounds in the playoffs

NLDS—National League Division Series, the first of three rounds in the playoffs

no-decision—a statistic that's given to a starting pitcher who neither wins nor loses

no-doubles defense—a type of defensive alignment designed to protect a small, late-game lead by making it harder for the batter to deliver an extra-base hit

no-doubter—a sure home run

no-hitter—a game in which the pitcher does not allow any hits

no-no—a no-hitter

non-tender—a player who is not offered a contract

nose to toes—describes the movement of a curveball that starts high and finishes low

nothing on it—describes a pitch with poor velocity or little movement

nubber—a weak ground ball that trickles a short distance from home plate

number one—a fastball

number two—a curveball

-O-

October—the postseason

off-balance throw—a throw on which the fielder does not plant his feet

off-speed pitch—a pitch that's thrown slower than the fastball

official scorer—the person who keeps track of the game's action and determines how it breaks down into various statistical categories; sometimes referred to as the official scorekeeper

ohfer—a hitless game or streak for a batter (literally "0-for")

on a fly—before it bounces

on deck—due to bat after the current hitter

on his horse—running full speed

on the black—barely wide of home plate (which has a black edge buried in the dirt)

on the interstate—batting below .200 (I-95, for example, looks like .195)

on the schneid—in a slump

on-base percentage—a statistic that shows how often the batter reaches base safely

on-deck circle—the area between home plate and the dugout where the on-deck hitter awaits his turn to bat

one away—one out

one-hopper—a ball that bounces once before reaching the fielder

one-two-three inning—an inning in which all three hitters make consecutive outs

open base—an unoccupied base behind the runner

opposite field—left field for a left-handed hitter or right field for a right-handed hitter

optioned—demoted from the Major Leagues to the Minor Leagues

organization—a major league team and its minor league affiliates

out of play—out of bounds or inactive

out-pitch—a pitcher's best pitch, which he uses to finish off the hitter

outer half—the space between the middle of the strike zone and the outer edge of home plate

over .500—more wins than losses

overshift—a defensive alignment used against powerful left-handed pull-hitters

-P-

paint the corner—to throw a pitch over the edge of home plate

palmball—a change-up

parachute—a weak fly ball between the infielders and outfielders

parent club—the major league team within an organization

parking place—an open base

passed ball—a pitch that should have been caught by the catcher and that allows a runner to advance

payoff pitch—the pitch with three balls and two strikes

pea—a ball traveling at a high speed

pearl—a brand-new baseball

peeker—a hitter with a reputation for looking back at the catcher to steal his signs or location

'pen—the bullpen

pennant—the league championship

pepper—a practice game in which a small group of players take turns pitching lightly to one guy who taps grounders back to them from 20 or 30 feet away

perfect game—a game in which the pitcher does not allow anyone to reach base

phantom tag—a tag that barely misses the runner but tricks the umpire into calling an out

piano mover—a slow runner

pick it—to catch a short hop

pick up the ball—to see the ball

pickle—a rundown

pickoff—a throw toward a base where the runner takes his lead

pinch-hit—to bat in place of another hitter

pinch-run—to run in place of another runner

pine tar—a sticky substance that gives the hitter a better grip on his bat

pitch around—to throw pitches just outside the strike zone (rather than issuing an intentional walk) to lure the batter into swinging at a ball

pitcher of record—the pitcher who will get the decision if the lead doesn't change hands

pitcher's best friend—a double play

pitcher's park—a field that favors the defense because of its large dimensions

pitcher's pitch—a pitch thrown exactly how the pitcher intended it

pitchers' duel—a low-scoring game

pitchout—a fastball thrown intentionally high and outside to give the catcher an unobstructed chance to catch the ball and throw out a runner who's trying to steal a base

plate appearance—a turn at bat

plate coverage—the batter's ability to hit both inside and outside pitches

platooned—forced to share playing time at one position

play under protest—to continue playing after formally objecting to an umpire's misapplication of the rules

player to be named later—a player who's involved in a trade but not yet agreed upon when the teams announce the rest of the deal

player's manager—a manager who's laid-back and gets along with everyone on the team

plunked—hit by a pitch

plus—indicates that a pitcher pitched to at least one hitter in a new inning but didn't record any outs

pop—power

pop-up slide—a foot-first slide that helps the runner get back on his feet

position player—a nonpitcher

power alley—the distance to the wall in left- and right-center field

power hitter—a batter who hits lots of home runs

power pitcher—a pitcher who relies on his above-average fastball

protect the plate—to swing defensively with two strikes in order to make contact

protect the runner—to make contact (or at least swing) when the runner takes off

pull-hitter—a batter who rarely hits the ball to the opposite field

pull the ball—to swing slightly early and hit the pitch before it reaches home plate; a righty pulls the ball toward left field and a lefty pulls it toward the right side

pull the string—to throw a curveball

pull the trigger—to swing

Punch 'n' Judy—a hitter with little power

punched out—called out on strikes

purpose-pitch—a high and inside fastball that's intended to intimidate the hitter and make him back away from home plate on the next pitch

putout—a statistic awarded to a fielder who records an out by catching a batted ball on a fly, tagging a runner, or stepping on a base for a force play

-Q-

Quadruple-A—a hypothetical level of play between Triple-A and the Major Leagues

quality start—a game in which the starting pitcher lasts at least six innings and surrenders three or fewer earned runs

QuesTec—a device that's used by Major League Baseball officials to judge umpires based on how accurately they call balls and strikes

quick-pitch—to throw a pitch before the batter or runner is ready

-R-

rabbit—a knuckleball

rabbit ears—a short-tempered umpire who hears everything bad said about him

rain-maker—an incredibly high pop-up

raked—hit hard

rally—a burst of offense for the team that's losing

rally cap—a baseball cap that's worn in a funny way in hopes of bringing good luck and helping a team score runs

range—a fielder's ability to move from side to side

RBI—runs batted in

reach back—to throw a fastball harder than normal

real estate—the area that an outfielder must cover

recalled—promoted from the Minor Leagues to the Major Leagues

receiver—the catcher

regular season—the 162-game schedule between Spring Training and the playoffs

rehab assignment—a short stint in the Minor Leagues to recover from an injury

rent-a-player—a player who gets traded to a contending team for the last two months of the season and then signs a contract with a different team as soon as he becomes a free agent

retired—to be put out by the fielding team

rib-eyes—ribbies

ribbies—runs batted in (the literal pronunciation of "RBIs")

rifle—a strong throwing arm

ring—a World Series ring, given to the members of a championship team

rising fastball—a fastball that stays high as it passes through the strike zone

roll one over—to hit a ground ball

rookie ball—the lowest of six levels in the Minor Leagues

room service hop—a bounce that is easy to catch because it lands well in front of the fielder

rope—a hard line drive

rotation—a team's starting pitchers

rotator cuff—the muscle group that stabilizes the shoulder joint

Rotisserie baseball—fantasy baseball; originally named "Rotisserie" because the guy who invented it (a famous baseball writer named Dan Okrent) used to play it with his friends at a New York City restaurant called La Rotisserie Francaise

roundtripper—a home run

rubber—the white rectangular slab against which the pitcher must place one foot before throwing the ball

rubber arm—the arm of a relief pitcher who can pitch day after day without getting tired

rubber game—the final game of a tied series

rug—AstroTurf or any other artificial playing surface

Rule 5 Draft—an annual, off-season draft of players who are already in the Minor Leagues

run his hands up—to move the hands on the bat before bunting

run support—the number of runs a team scores for its own pitcher

rundown—a play in which the runner gets caught between bases

rung up—called out on strikes

runner's box—the 45-foot lane in which the batter must run to avoid blocking a throw on his way to first base; marked with chalk and located just outside the foul line

runners on the corners—runners on first and third base

runs batted in—an offensive statistic that records how many runs score as a result of the batter's performance

runway—the corridor that connects the dugout to the concourse beneath the stands

-S-

sac bunt—a sacrifice bunt

sac fly—a sacrifice fly

sacrifice bunt—a bunt on which the hitter willingly gets thrown out at first base in order to advance a runner

sacrifice fly—a fly ball that gets caught and enables a runner to score

safety—a single

safety squeeze—a cautious version of the squeeze play in which the runner on third base doesn't race toward home plate until the ball has been bunted

salary cap—a rule in other sports that limits teams' payrolls

save—a statistic awarded to a relief pitcher on the winning team who finishes the game and preserves a small lead (usually three runs or fewer)

scoring position—on second or third base

scratched—removed from the starting lineup shortly before the game

screamer—a hard line drive

screwball—a pitch that moves in the opposite direction of a curveball

scroogie—a screwball

second cleanup hitter—a mock nickname for the eighth batter in the lineup

secondary lead—the extra steps that a runner takes as the pitcher releases the ball

seed—a ball traveling at a high speed

seeing-eye single—a slow ground ball that sneaks past a couple of infielders

send down—to demote a player from the Major Leagues to the Minor Leagues

Senior Circuit—the National League (which formed in 1876, 25 years before the American League)

sent to the showers—ejected from the game

set—the set position

set position—the pause before the pitch when the pitcher is trying to prevent the runner from taking a big lead

set the table—to get on base at the start of an inning

set-up man—a relief pitcher who tries to preserve the lead for the closer

seventh-inning stretch—a traditional break in the action in the middle of the seventh inning

shade—to position oneself slightly to the left or right when playing defense

shag—1. to practice fielding fly balls 2. to collect balls during batting practice

shake off—to disagree with the catcher's pitch selection

shelled—describes a pitcher who gives up lots of hits

shineball—a spitball

shoestring catch—a running catch that's made just before the ball hits the ground

short hop—a ball that bounces very close to the fielder

short leash—1. refers to a pitcher who'll probably get taken out of the game if he allows another batter to reach base 2. a limited pitch count

short porch—a section of outfield seats that's close to home plate

shorten up—1. to choke up 2. to take a quick, controlled swing

shovel—to make a short underhand toss while moving toward the target

Show, The—the Major Leagues

shutout—a game in which one team doesn't score

Silver Slugger Award—the annual award for the best hitter at each position in each league

simulated game—a throwing session (for a pitcher recovering from an injury) that duplicates the approximate pace of a game

Single-A—the third lowest of six levels in the Minor Leagues

sinker—a pitch that drops as it reaches the batter

sit dead red—to expect a fastball

situational hitting—the ability to advance a runner by hitting the ball to a certain spot

sit on a fastball—to expect a fastball

situational lefty—a left-handed relief pitcher who faces just one or two left-handed batters per game

skin—the dirt-covered area of the infield

skipper—the manager

slab—the pitching rubber

slam range—four runs or less

slap-hitter—a left-handed batter who takes short, compact swings and often hits the ball to the opposite field

slice the ball—to hit the ball to the opposite field

slide piece—a slider

slide step—a small stride toward home plate on which the pitcher barely lifts his foot

slider—a pitch that combines the movement of a fastball and a curveball

slop—a steady flow of off-speed pitches

slugfest—a high-scoring game

slugging percentage—a statistic that measures the batter's skill at delivering extra-base hits

slump—an extended period of poor hitting

slurve—a pitch that combines the movement of a slider and a curveball

small ball—a style of play in which the offensive team uses basic fundamentals to advance its runners one or two bases at a time

small-market team—a team that is located in a small city and, because of its limited fan base, has less money to spend on players

smart ball—a less derogatory term for small ball, coined by White Sox manager Ozzie Guillen during his team's championship run in 2005

smoke—a fastball

snap throw—a sudden pick-off throw

snapper—a curveball

snatch catch—a catch in which the outfielder swats at the ball with his glove

snow cone—a catch in which the ball lands in (or squirts to) the tip of the glove and pokes out like a scoop of vanilla ice cream

soft-toss—a hitting drill during which the batter hits lightly tossed balls into a net

softball numbers—incredible batting statistics

solo home run—a home run with no one on base

sophomore slump—a bad second season after a great rookie season

southpaw—a left-handed player

specialist—a situational lefty

spiked—injured by spikes

spikes—the pointy metal shoe bottoms that help players get good traction

Spink Award—the award for sportswriters who get inducted to the Hall of Fame

spitball—a now-illegal pitch that pitchers used to throw by applying saliva (or any other greasy substance) to the ball and squirting it out of their hands upon release

split-finger fastball—a fastball that drops as it reaches the batter

splitter—a split-finger fastball

splitty—a split-finger fastball

spoiler—a lousy team that beats a postseason contender late in the season

spot a fastball—to hit the catcher's target with a fastball

spot starter—a pitcher who occasionally starts a game

spray chart—a diagram that shows the direction of a batter's hits

spray-hitter—a batter who hits to all fields with little power

Spring Training—preseason

square around—to get in position to bunt by turning to face the pitcher

squeeze—1. the squeeze play 2. to call a "ball" on a pitch that's close to the strike zone

squeeze play—an offensive play designed to score a runner from third with a bunt

squibber—a ground ball that's hit off the end of the bat and trickles slowly with lots of spin

stand-up double—a double on which the batter does not slide into second base

starter—the first pitcher of the game

station-to-station—one base at a time

step in the bucket—to step away from home plate in fear of being hit by the pitch

Steve Blass Disease—a psychological condition that results in a player's total loss of throwing accuracy; named after a successful Pirates pitcher who inexplicably melted down after the 1972 season

stick it in his back pocket—to hold the ball instead of throwing it

stolen base percentage—a statistic that shows how often the runner succeeds when he tries to steal a base

stopper—the final relief pitcher who tries to preserve the lead

straight steal—a stolen base without the use of another play or strategy

straightaway—standard defensive positioning

stranded—left on base at the end of an inning

stretch—a shortened delivery, which the pitcher uses with a runner on base

strike-'em-out/throw-'em-out double play—a double play that's made by throwing out a base stealer on a pitch that struck out the hitter

stuff—the pitcher's movement, velocity, and overall ability

submariner—a pitcher who throws with such an extreme sidearm motion that it almost looks like he's underhanding the ball

suicide squeeze—an aggressive version of the squeeze play in which the runner on third base breaks toward home plate before the pitch

Sunday hop—a bounce that's easy to catch because it lands well in front of the fielder

sweep—to win every game in a series

sweet spot—1. the part of the bat that hits the ball hardest 2. the spot on a baseball, opposite the logo, where autograph collectors prefer star players to sign

swifty—a fastball

swing from the heels—to swing the bat extremely hard

swinging bunt—a batted ball that is hit weakly and rolls like a bunt

swingman—a pitcher who's used as both a starter and a reliever

switch-hitter—a hitter who can bat right- or left-handed

-T-

tag—1. to retire a base runner by touching him with the ball 2. to tag up

tag up—to advance to the next base after a batted ball has been caught on a fly

tailing fastball—a fastball that moves laterally—toward a righty if thrown by a righty—as it reaches the batter

tailor-made—easy to field

take a lead—to get a head start by moving several steps off the base before the pitch is thrown

take a pitch—to let a pitch go by instead of swinging at it

take one for the team—1. to intentionally get hit by a pitch (the batter must do it subtly because it's illegal) 2. to pitch through a miserable performance in order to let the bullpen rest

takeout slide—a slide in which the runner collides with a fielder to prevent him from making another throw

take sign—instructions to let a pitch go by instead of swinging at it

take something off—to throw a pitch slower than the one before

tank—to make an error

tape-measure shot—a long home run

tater—a home run

Ted Williams shift—a defensive alignment used against powerful, left-handed pull-hitters

10/5 player—a player who has the right to veto any trade because he's spent at least ten years in the Major Leagues and five consecutive seasons with his current team

Texas Leaguer—a weak fly ball that drops between the infielders and outfielders

textbook—mechanically perfect

30/30 club—the group of players who have hit at least 30 home runs and stolen at least 30 bases in one season

thread the needle—to pitch with perfect accuracy

three days' rest—one day short of the typical time off between games for a starting pitcher

three-quarters—the arm angle between overhand and sidearm

three up, three down—describes an inning in which three batters make consecutive outs

through the wickets—through the legs

throw behind the runner—to throw the ball to a base just after the runner has passed it

throw the kitchen sink—to throw a wacky pitch (or combination of pitches) in a desperate attempt to retire the hitter

throw through—to throw the ball from home plate to second base when it could be thrown elsewhere

tip the pitch—to accidentally reveal what type of pitch is coming

toe the rubber—to touch the rubber before throwing a pitch

tomahawk—1. to hit a high pitch 2. to swing at a downward angle and hit the top of the ball

Tommy John surgery—elbow surgery

tools of ignorance—catcher's equipment

top out—to reach one's top pitch speed

total bases—the number of bases that the batter reaches by hitting the ball

total chances—a fielder's combined number of putouts, assists, and errors

touch 'em all—to circle the bases after hitting a home run

tough save—a save in which the pitcher enters the game with the tying run on base

trademark—the weak part of the bat between the handle and barrel

trading deadlines—deadlines for trading players and establishing postseason rosters

trail runner—the runner who's farther from home plate

transaction—the addition or removal of a player from a team's roster

trap—to catch a fly ball or line drive just after it hits the ground

Triple-A—the highest of six levels in the Minor Leagues

Triple Crown—the award for a batter who leads his league in home runs, runs batted in, and batting average, or for a pitcher who leads his league in wins, strikeouts, and earned run average

triple play—a single play on which the fielding team records three outs

true rookie—a player with absolutely no major league experience prior to the current season

tumbler—a curveball that doesn't curve

tunnel—the concourse beneath the stands that leads to the clubhouses, batting cages, umpires' room, and other key areas

Turface—a sandlike material used by groundskeepers to absorb water on the infield dirt

turn him loose—to give a batter permission to swing with three balls and no strikes

turn on the ball—to pull the ball

turn two—to execute a double play

'tweener—a player who excels in the Minor Leagues but isn't quite talented enough to find a regular job in the majors

12-to-6—describes a curveball that starts high and finishes low (picture the numbers 12 and 6 on a clock)

twi-night doubleheader—a doubleheader that starts in the late afternoon or evening

twin bill—a doubleheader

twin killing—a double play

two-seam fastball—a type of fastball that moves laterally as it reaches the batter

two-seamer—a two-seam fastball

-U-

unassisted triple play—a triple play that's made without a throw

unbalanced schedule—a schedule (currently used by Major League Baseball) in which teams don't all face each other the same number of times during the season

Uncle Charlie—a curveball

under .500—more losses than wins

unintentional intentional walk—a standard (but premeditated) walk that's issued by throwing pitches just outside the strike zone in case the batter swings at a bad pitch

up the elevator shaft—directly above home plate

up the middle—toward center field

uppercut—an attempt to hit a home run by swinging with an upward angle

utilityman—a part-time player who fills in at several positions

-V-

veteran—a player who's been in the Major Leagues for a long time

Veterans Committee—a group of Hall of Famers who help decide which players get inducted into the Hall of Fame after their 15-year eligibility expires

virtual tie—a situation in which two (or more) teams are tied in the standings despite having slightly different winning percentages

vulture—a relief pitcher who wins a lot of games

-W-

waivers—a tactic used by team management to dump an unwanted player

walk-off home run—a game-winning home run in the bottom of the ninth or in extra innings

walking lead—a lead in which the base runner gains momentum before running by timing the pitcher's delivery and taking a few steps

warning track—the dirt lane around the edge of the field

warning track power—an insult for a hitter whose deep fly ball falls short of the wall

waste-pitch—a pitch that's intentionally thrown for a ball

wheel play—a defensive play that's used to thwart a sacrifice bunt with a runner on second

wheelhouse—the location within the strike zone where the batter hits with most power

wheels—running speed

whiff—to strike out

Wild Card—the postseason berth for the best second-place team in each league

wild pitch—a pitch that misses the catcher's target by such a wide margin that the ball gets loose and allows a base runner to advance

wild within the strike zone—able to throw strikes, but unable to hit the catcher's specific target

windup—a complex series of movements (small step backward, pivot, leg kick, push off the rubber, stride, and release) that precedes the pitch

winning percentage—a statistic that shows how often a team, pitcher, or manager wins

work the count—to prolong the at-bat by fouling off strikes and not swinging at balls

work up a lather—to warm up quickly in the bullpen

workhorse—a pitcher who throws a lot of innings

World Baseball Classic—an international tournament that takes place every four years

World Series—the final round of the postseason

worm-burner—a ground ball that takes many small bounces

-Y-

yakker—a curveball

yardwork!—home run!

MORE STATISTICS

That's Hendrick's 19th home run. One more and he reaches double figures.

—Jerry Coleman, Hall-of-Fame announcer

These are the most important baseball stats along with their abbreviations and the single-season and career records:

BATTING		SINGLE-SEASON	CAREER
G	games played	165—Maury Wills, 1962	3,562—Pete Rose
AB	at-bats	705—Willie Wilson, 1980	14,053—Pete Rose
PA	plate appearances	773—Lenny Dykstra, 1993	15,861—Pete Rose
H	hits	262—Ichiro Suzuki, 2004	4,256—Pete Rose
1B	singles	225—Ichiro Suzuki, 2004	3,215—Pete Rose
2B	doubles	67—Earl Webb, 1931	792—Tris Speaker
3B	triples	36—Chief Wilson, 1912	309—Sam Crawford
HR	home runs	73—Barry Bonds, 2001	755—Hank Aaron
AB/HR	home run ratio	6.52—Barry Bonds, 2001	10.80—Mark McGwire
GS	grand slams	6—two players tied[1]	23—Lou Gehrig
AVG	batting average	.440—Hugh Duffy, 1894	.367—Ty Cobb
SLG	slugging percentage	.863—Barry Bonds, 2001	.690—Babe Ruth
OBP	on-base percentage	.609—Barry Bonds, 2004	.483—Ted Williams
OPS	on-base plus slugging	1.422—Barry Bonds, 2004	1.164—Babe Ruth

(continued)

[1]Don Mattingly (1987) and Travis Hafner (2006)

		SINGLE-SEASON	CAREER
TB	total bases	457—Babe Ruth, 1921	6,856—Hank Aaron
XBH	extra-base hits	119—Babe Ruth, 1921	1,477—Hank Aaron
R	runs	192—Billy Hamilton, 1894	2,295—Rickey Henderson
RBI	runs batted in	191—Hack Wilson, 1930	2,297—Hank Aaron
SO	strikeouts	195—Adam Dunn, 2004	2,597—Reggie Jackson
BB	bases on balls	232—Barry Bonds, 2004	2,426—Barry Bonds
IBB	intentional bases on balls	120—Barry Bonds, 2004	645—Barry Bonds
HP	hit by pitch	51—Hughie Jennings, 1896	287—Hughie Jennings
SB	stolen bases	130—Rickey Henderson, 1982	1,406—Rickey Henderson
CS	caught stealing	42—Rickey Henderson, 1982	335—Rickey Henderson
PH	pinch hits	28—John Vander Wal, 1995	212—Lenny Harris
SAC	sacrifice bunts	67—Ray Chapman, 1917	512—Eddie Collins
SF	sacrifice flies	19—Gil Hodges, 1954	128—Eddie Murray
GIDP	grounded into double play	36—Jim Rice, 1984	350—Cal Ripken Jr.

PITCHING		SINGLE-SEASON	CAREER
W	wins	41—Jack Chesbro, 1904	511—Cy Young
L	losses	35—Red Donahue, 1897	316—Cy Young
PCT	winning percentage	.947—Roy Face, 1959	.717—Spud Chandler
G	games pitched	106—Mike Marshall, 1974	1,252—Jesse Orosco
GS	games started	52—Amos Rusie, 1893	815—Cy Young
CG	complete games	50—Amos Rusie, 1893	749—Cy Young
IP	innings pitched	482—Amos Rusie, 1893	7,356—Cy Young
SO	strikeouts	383—Nolan Ryan, 1973	5,714—Nolan Ryan
K/9	strikeouts per 9 IP	13.41—Randy Johnson, 2001	10.77—Randy Johnson
BB	bases on balls	218—Amos Rusie, 1893	2,795—Nolan Ryan
WP	wild pitches	30—Red Ames, 1905	277—Nolan Ryan
BK	balks	16—Dave Stewart, 1988	90—Steve Carlton
HB	hit batsmen	40—Joe McGinnity, 1900	219—Chick Fraser
H	hits allowed	497—Ted Breitenstein, 1894	7,092—Cy Young
HR	home runs allowed	50—Bert Blyleven, 1986	505—Robin Roberts
R	runs allowed	320—Ted Breitenstein, 1894	3,167—Cy Young
ER	earned runs allowed	238—Ted Breitenstein, 1894	2,147—Cy Young

(continued)

PITCHING		SINGLE-SEASON	CAREER
ERA	earned run average	0.96—Dutch Leonard, 1914	1.82—Ed Walsh
SH	shutouts	16—Grover "Pete" Alexander, 1916	110—Walter Johnson
SV	saves	57—Bobby Thigpen, 1990	482—Trevor Hoffman
BS	blown saves	14—four players tied[2]	112—Rich Gossage
WHIP	walks + hits per inning	0.74—Pedro Martinez, 2000	0.97—Addie Joss

Many other stats never reach the scoreboard or your television because they're obscure or specific to one-of-a-kind situations. Still, it's good to know that they exist.

HITTING

- **PAB (pinch-hit at-bats)**—This is a dubious record to own because it means that the player wasn't good enough to be in the starting lineup.

- **RISP (runners in scoring position)**—When you read that your favorite team is "batting .083 with RISP," you'll understand why they've lost 14 games in a row.

- **LIPS (late-inning pressure situations)**—A manager can use this stat to determine which hitter he should use with RISP late in the game.

- **LOB (number of runners left on base)**—Whether a runner gets stranded or erased on a double play, the hitter (or the team as a whole) is held responsible for having left him on base. But is it always the hitter's fault? Joe Torre didn't think so in 1975 when, as an infielder with the Mets, he bounced into four double plays in one game, each time wiping out Felix Millan, who batted in front of

---

[2]Rollie Fingers (1976), Bruce Sutter (1978), Bob Stanley (1983), and Ron Davis (1984).

him and went 4-for-4. "What's everyone blaming me for?" Torre complained afterward. "Blame Felix. I wouldn't have hit into the double plays if he hadn't hit singles."

- **RMU (runners moved up)**—Base hits technically move up the runners. So do walks and sac bunts and lots of other things, but this stat specifically means: runners moved up by having grounded out.

- **NP/PA (number of pitches seen per plate appearance)**—The more the better. When a batter goes deep in the count, he wears out the pitcher and increases his chance of drawing a walk.

- **PA/SO (plate appearances per strikeout)**—In 1932 Yankees third baseman Joe Sewell *whiffed* just three times all season for an incredible ratio of 192:1.

- **G/F (ground ball/fly ball ratio)**—If the ratio leans heavily one way, the hitter might be asked to show up for early BP.

- **IsoP (isolated power)**—Easy to calculate: just subtract batting average from slugging percentage.

- **SB% (stolen base percentage)**—If a runner doesn't succeed at least 75 percent of the time, he's not helping his team.

PITCHING

- **QS (quality starts)**—A pitcher gets credit when he throws at least six innings and allows three or fewer earned runs.

- **I/GS (innings pitched per game started)**—In this overprotective era, six or seven is considered great.

- **RS (run support)**—Bo Belinsky, a pitcher in the 1960s, once said, "How can a guy win a game if you don't give him any runs?" It was an excellent point (except for the fact that he'd just lost, 15–0). This stat measures how many runs per game the team averages for each pitcher.

- **K/BB (strikeout/walk ratio)**—A good pitcher will average at least two strikeouts for every walk. In 1994 Mets starter Bret Saberhagen posted an 11:1 ratio and had fewer walks than wins!

- **BB/9 (walks per nine innings)**—Although there's a separate category for intentional walks, they're also counted in the regular walk tally and therefore figure into this ratio. A good pitcher walks fewer than three batters per game.

- **H/9 (hits per nine innings)**—Pitchers with excellent control sometimes give up lots of hits because their pitches are often in or near the strike zone. Greg Maddux is a great example.

- **CGL (complete-game losses)**—You won't see too many of these. Nowadays, pitchers rarely throw nine innings even when they're winning.

- **OBA (opponents' batting average)**—The best pitchers keep their opponents below .200.

- **NP (number of pitches thrown)**—Twenty pitches per inning is lousy. Fifteen is good. Ten is amazing.

- **BF (total batters faced)**—When you read the box score, don't be impressed just because a guy faced 34 batters; he might have pitched just two innings.

- **PK (pickoffs)**—This is more of a fielding stat, but pitchers are the only players who officially get credit for them. Lefties always lead the league.

- **XBA (extra-base hits allowed)**—Few people use this stat. It's better to judge a pitcher based on how many home runs he surrenders.

- **IRA (inherited runs allowed)**—When a reliever enters the game with men on base, it's not fair to penalize his earned run average if they score. That's why IRA was invented. Unfortunately, like most stats, it fails to weigh the circumstances; did he enter the game with two outs and a man on first or no outs and a runner on third?

- **RW (relief wins)**—Getting a win in relief is based less on skill than on the luck of the situation. *Vultures,* of course, would argue otherwise.

- **SVO (save opportunities)**—The best closers convert more than 85 percent of their opportunities to saves. Eric Gagne succeeded a record 84 times in a row for the Dodgers from 2002 to 2004. He was so dominant that the scoreboard operator flashed GAME OVER whenever he trotted in from the bullpen.

- **HLD (holds)**—Awarded to a pitcher who gets at least one out and preserves a midgame lead in a save situation, this statistic was invented in 1999 to give middle relievers the recognition they deserve—and something to brag about in arbitration. In case you care (and you shouldn't), Tom Gordon and Scott Linebrink share the single-season record with 36.

- **ND (no-decisions)**—A decision is a win or loss for a pitcher. A starter gets a no-decision when he leaves the game with the score tied or when the lead changes hands after he's gone—or if he has the lead and leaves before completing five innings.

- **GF (games finished)**—Don't confuse this with complete games. This simply records who retired the final batter.

FIELDING

- **INN (innings played)**—Statisticians began keeping track in 1999.

- **TC (total chances)**—A fielder gets a chance by touching the ball when he's expected to make an out. If, for example, the first baseman catches a pick-off throw, it's not a chance (unless he actually tags out the runner or makes an error) because he can't be charged with an error if the runner is not retired. If, however, he handles a routine pop-up, he does get a chance.

- **PO (putouts)**—There are three main ways for a fielder to get a putout: catching a batted ball on a fly, tagging out a runner, and stepping on a base for a force-out. In addition, the catcher gets a putout on every strike-out (except when he drops the third strike and has to throw out the runner at first). And when the runner gets hit by a batted ball in fair territory, the fielder standing closest to him gets the putout. Not too many people know this.

- **A (assists)**—A fielder gets an assist when he records an out by throwing the ball. Even though the catcher gets a putout on a strikeout, the pitcher does not get an assist. (That doesn't seem fair, does it?)

- **OFA (outfield assists)**—While infielders record hundreds of assists per season, 10 is an excellent total for an outfielder. Tris Speaker, a legendary center fielder who in 1937 became the seventh player elected to the Hall of Fame, holds both the single-season (35) and career record (449).

- **E (errors)**—In 1890 Billy Shindle, the shortstop for the Philadelphia Quakers of the Players League,[3] made 119 errors—but the fields weren't too good back then.

- **FA (fielding average)**—Billy Shindle's fielding average was so ugly that it frightened small children.

- **DP (double plays)**—Mickey Vernon, a first baseman who played from 1939 to 1960, holds the career record with 2,044.

- **TP (triple plays)**—Most players go their entire careers without participating in a triple play.

- **CS% (caught stealing percentage)**—The best catchers nail approximately one-third of would-be base stealers.

- **PB (passed balls)**—Passed balls do not count as errors and therefore have no effect on fielding average.

- **CERA (catcher's earned run average)**—No, catchers don't pitch. This stat keeps track of a pitching staff's earned run average while a particular catcher is behind the plate.

[3]In 1889 there were two major leagues: the National League and the American Association. The Players League was created the following year to compete with them, but it didn't last beyond its first season. (Perhaps some of the team names are to blame. Would *you* have paid to watch the Pittsburgh Burghers battle the Cleveland Infants?) The American Association didn't last long either, hanging on from 1882 to 1891. The Union Association (1884) and Federal League (1914–15) are the only other defunct major leagues.

APPENDIX B
UNIFORM NUMBERS

A lot of long relievers are ashamed to tell their parents what they do. The only nice thing about it is that you get to wear a uniform like everybody else.

—Jim Bouton, former major league pitcher

Note: Players who switched numbers appear just once on the list, next to the number they wore most.

1—Richie Ashburn (OF), Jim Bottomley (1B), Earle Combs (OF), Bobby Doerr (2B), Tony Fernandez (SS), Rabbit Maranville (SS), Billy Martin (M), Bill McKechnie (M), Pee Wee Reese (SS), Ozzie Smith (SS), Lou Whitaker (2B)

2—Leo Durocher (M), Nellie Fox (2B), Charlie Gehringer (2B), Billy Herman (2B), Derek Jeter (SS), Tommy Lasorda (M), Red Schoendienst (2B)

3—Earl Averill (OF), Harold Baines (OF/DH), Mickey Cochrane (C), Kiki Cuyler (OF), Jimmie Foxx (1B), Frankie Frisch (2B), Harmon Killebrew (1B/3B), Chuck Klein (OF), Heinie Manush (OF), Dale Murphy (OF), Edgar Renteria (SS), Alex Rodriguez (SS/3B), Babe Ruth (OF/P), Bill Terry (1B), Alan Trammell (SS)

4—Luke Appling (SS), Joe Cronin (SS), Lou Gehrig (1B), Goose Goslin (OF), Chick Hafey (OF), Rogers

Hornsby (2B), Ralph Kiner (OF), Ernie Lombardi (C), Paul Molitor (3B/DH), Mel Ott (OF), Duke Snider (OF), Miguel Tejada (SS), Earl Weaver (M), Hack Wilson (OF)

5—Jeff Bagwell (1B), Johnny Bench (C), Lou Boudreau (SS/M), George Brett (3B), Joe DiMaggio (OF), Nomar Garciaparra (SS), Hank Greenberg (1B), Travis Jackson (SS), Albert Pujols (1B/3B/OF), Brooks Robinson (3B), David Wright (3B)

6—Bobby Cox (M), Steve Garvey (1B), Ryan Howard (1B), Al Kaline (OF), Tony Lazzeri (2B), Stan Musial (OF/1B), Tony Oliva (OF), Johnny Pesky (SS/3B), Joe Torre (C/1B/M), Willie Wilson (OF)

7—Craig Biggio (2B), George Kell (3B), Kenny Lofton (OF), Mickey Mantle (OF), Joe Mauer (C), Joe Medwick (OF), Jose Reyes (SS), Ivan Rodriguez (C), Al Simmons (OF)

8—Albert Belle (OF), Yogi Berra (C), Gary Carter (C), Doc Cramer (OF), Bill Dickey (C), Rick Ferrell (C), Joe Morgan (2B), Cal Ripken Jr. (SS), Willie Stargell (OF/1B), Carl Yastrzemski (OF)

9—Bob Boone (C), Gabby Hartnett (C), Roger Maris (OF), Bill Mazeroski (2B), Minnie Minoso (OF), Graig Nettles (3B), Juan Pierre (OF), Enos Slaughter (OF), Bob Uecker (C), Ted Williams (OF)

10—Larry Bowa (SS/M), Andre Dawson (OF), Lefty Grove (P), Chipper Jones (3B), Tony La Russa (M), Johnny Mize (1B), Phil Rizzuto (SS), Ron Santo (3B), Gary Sheffield (OF), Rusty Staub (OF), Lloyd Waner (OF), Michael Young (SS)

11—Sparky Anderson (M), Luis Aparicio (SS), Lefty Gomez (P), Carl Hubbell (P), Barry Larkin (SS), Edgar Martinez (DH), Hal McRae (DH), Jimmy Rollins (SS), Paul Waner (OF)

12—Roberto Alomar (2B), Dusty Baker (OF/M), Steve Finley (OF), Jeff Kent (2B), Freddie Lindstrom (3B/OF), Alfonso Soriano (2B)

13—Dave Concepcion (SS), Carl Crawford (OF), Ozzie Guillen (SS/M), Lance Parrish (C), Omar Vizquel (SS), Billy Wagner (P)

14—Ernie Banks (1B/SS), Ken Boyer (3B), Jim Bunning (P), Larry Doby (OF), Julio Franco (SS/2B), Gil Hodges (1B), George Kelly (1B), Lou Piniella (OF/M), Jim Rice (OF), Pete Rose (OF/1B/3B/2B)

15—Dick Allen (1B/3B), Carlos Beltran (OF), Jim Edmonds (OF), Shawn Green (OF), Tim Hudson (P), Thurman Munson (C), Red Ruffing (P), Dazzy Vance (P)

16—Whitey Ford (P), Jason Giambi (1B), Dwight Gooden (P), Jesse Haines (P), Ted Lyons (P), Hal Newhouser (P), Al Oliver (OF), Herb Pennock (P), Reggie Sanders (OF)

17—Lance Berkman (OF), Dizzy Dean (P), Mark Grace (1B), Todd Helton (1B), Keith Hernandez (1B), Scott Rolen (3B)

18—Moises Alou (OF), Johnny Damon (OF), Red Faber (P), Mel Harder (P), Jason Kendall (C), Ted Kluszewski (1B), Eppa Rixey (P), Darryl Strawberry (OF)

19—Bob Feller (P), Juan Gonzalez (OF), Tony Gwynn (OF), Robin Yount (SS/OF)

20—Burleigh Grimes (P), Monte Irvin (OF), Mark Mulder (P), Frank Robinson (OF/M), Mike Schmidt (3B), Don Sutton (P), Pie Traynor (3B), Frank White (2B)

21—Lou Brock (OF), Spud Chandler (P), Roger Clemens (P), Roberto Clemente (OF), Bob Lemon (P), Joe Sewell (SS/3B), Sammy Sosa (OF), Warren Spahn (P), Arky Vaughan (SS)

22—Bill Buckner (1B), Harry Heilmann (OF), Jim Palmer (P), Allie Reynolds (P), Sam Rice (OF)

23—Felipe Alou (OF/M), Don Mattingly (1B), Ryne Sandberg (2B), Ted Simmons (C), Mark Teixeira (1B), Luis Tiant (P)

24—Walter Alston (M), Miguel Cabrera (OF/3B), Dwight Evans (OF), Ken Griffey Jr. (OF), Rickey Henderson (OF), Willie Mays (OF), Tony Perez (1B/3B), Manny Ramirez (OF/DH), Grady Sizemore (OF), Early Wynn (P)

25—Don Baylor (DH/OF), Buddy Bell (3B), Barry Bonds (OF), Bobby Bonds (OF), Carlos Delgado (1B), Frank Howard (OF), Tommy John (P), Andruw Jones (OF), Mark McGwire (1B), Rafael Palmeiro (1B/DH), Jim Thome (1B)

26—Wade Boggs (3B), Dave Kingman (OF/1B), Billy Williams (OF)

27—Kevin Brown (P), Carlton Fisk (C), Vladimir Guerrero (OF), Catfish Hunter (P), Juan Marichal (P)

28—Bert Blyleven (P), Sparky Lyle (P), Randy Myers (P), Vada Pinson (OF)

29—Rod Carew (1B/2B), Chris Carpenter (P), Joe Carter (OF), Mickey Lolich (P), Fred McGriff (1B), Satchel Paige (P), Dan Quisenberry (P), John Smoltz (P)

30—Orlando Cepeda (1B), Tim Raines (OF), Willie Randolph (2B/M), Mel Stottlemyre (P), Maury Wills (SS)

31—John Franco (P), Fergie Jenkins (P), Greg Maddux (P), Robb Nen (P), Mike Piazza (C), Hoyt Wilhelm (P), Dave Winfield (OF)

32—Steve Carlton (P), Roy Halladay (P), Sandy Koufax (P), Dennis Martinez (P)

33—Jose Canseco (OF/DH), Eddie Murray (1B), Larry Walker (OF), David Wells (P)

34—Rollie Fingers (P), David Ortiz (DH), Kirby Puckett (OF), Nolan Ryan (P), Fernando Valenzuela (P)

35—Mike Mussina (P), Phil Niekro (P), Frank Thomas (1B), John Wetteland (P), Dontrelle Willis (P)

36—David Cone (P), Jim Kaat (P), Joe Niekro (P), Gaylord Perry (P), Robin Roberts (P)

37—Casey Stengel (OF/M)

38—Eric Gagne (P), Curt Schilling (P), Carlos Zambrano (P)

39—Roy Campanella (C), Roberto Hernandez (P), Dave Parker (OF)

40—Bartolo Colon (P), Troy Percival (P), Frank Tanana (P)

41—Darrell Evans (3B/1B), Eddie Mathews (3B), Jeff Reardon (P), Tom Seaver (P)

42—Al Lopez (C/M), Mariano Rivera (P), Jackie Robinson (2B), Bruce Sutter (P), Mo Vaughn (1B)

43—Dennis Eckersley (P)

44—Hank Aaron (OF), Adam Dunn (OF), Reggie Jackson (OF), Willie McCovey (1B), Roy Oswalt (P)

45—Bob Gibson (P), Pedro Martinez (P)

46—Andy Pettitte (P), Lee Smith (P)

47—Tom Glavine (P), Jack Morris (P)

48—Travis Hafner (DH), Waite Hoyt (P)

49—Armando Benitez (P), Ron Guidry (P), Charlie Hough (P)

50—Bucky Harris (M), Tom Henke (P)

51—Trevor Hoffman (P), Randy Johnson (P), Willie McGee (OF), Ichiro Suzuki (OF), Bernie Williams (OF)

52—C. C. Sabathia (P)

53—Bobby Abreu (OF), Don Drysdale (P)

54—Rich Gossage (P)

55—Orel Hershiser (P), Hideki Matsui (OF)

With all due respect to Johan Santana (#57) and Barry Zito (#75), the list ends here because players with high numbers are usually pretty bad. (Tim Spooneybarger is, without a doubt, the best who ever wore number 91 but, with the exception of Mrs. Spooneybarger, there probably aren't too many people who care.) They're the minor leaguers who weren't expected to make it past Spring Training. Major leaguers occasionally keep their high numbers as badges of honor, but most guys eagerly ditch them for something more respectable.

ACKNOWLEDGMENTS

I'd like to start by thanking my parents, Stuart and Naomi, not only for being fabulous, but for being clueless enough about baseball to inspire this book.

There are others who helped tremendously, and Lia Norton belongs at the top of the list. She's so insightful and patient—and has done so much for the book over the last three years—that I could write an entire "acknowledgments" chapter about her.

Jules Owen generously took time away from his own writing to read an embarrassingly early draft of the manuscript, and in the true spirit of friendship, he never hesitated to point out all the places where it sucked. His guidance spanned the duration of this project and concluded with a last-minute reminder to add a paragraph about the gyroball.

Will Dodson (a crazy friend from Guilford College), Ben Greenwood (a sane friend from the SCRABBLE® world), and Brooke Linville (a wise friend from my writing group) also edited an early draft and gave invaluable suggestions. I didn't approach them. They offered. And the book wasn't even signed up.

Gillian MacKenzie made me feel like a champ from the moment we met and soon found a great home for the book. She has embraced all my geeky pursuits. She shares my hatred for a certain major league team. She's everything an agent should be.

Several people at Vintage should take a curtain call: Jenny Jackson, my editor, for being the voice of reason even when I was freaking out; Daniel Gillespie and Cathy Aison for taking a whole mess of fonts and headings and paragraphs and footnotes and charts and diagrams and making it pretty; Martin Wilson and Russell Perreault, not only for their publicity efforts, but for insisting that I order two desserts at our first lunch meeting; and Marty Asher for saying "yes" and overseeing it all.

Lots of other folks helped in less obvious ways, and since this book already has enough alphabetical lists, here they are in descending height order: George Amores, Ralph Carballal, Art Blount, Jeff Jeske, Mark Newman, Joe Kelly, Silke Kluever, Tim Leonard, Jason Ratliff, Carl Shimkin, Danny Polinsky, Harry Stein, Benjamin Hill, Dave Davis, Andrew Miller, Sean Heffron, Mike Miles, Bob Weil, Adam Stadlen, Olivia Todd, Steve Mandl, Rachel Eisenman, Byron Parkes, Pei Kang, Suzie Oh (who now hopefully knows what a ground ball is), and Naturi Thomas.